FOOLPROOF

VEGGIE
AIR FRYER

FOOLPROOF

VEGGIE AIR FRYER

60 SIMPLE AND SPEEDY
VEGETARIAN DISHES

LOUISE KENNEY

PHOTOGRAPHY BY
RITA PLATTS

Quadrille, Penguin Random House UK, One Embassy Gardens, 8 Viaduct Gardens, London SW11 7BW

Quadrille Publishing Limited is part of the Penguin Random House group of companies whose addresses can be found at global.penguinrandomhouse.com

Penguin
Random House
UK

Published by Quadrille in 2024

www.penguin.co.uk

A CIP catalogue record for this book is available from the British Library

ISBN 978 1837832163
10 9 8 7 6 5 4 3 2 1

Managing Director
Sarah Lavelle

Commissioning Editor
Stacey Cleworth

Project Editor
Harriet Webster

Series Designer
Emily Lapworth

Designer
Katy Everett

Photographer
Rita Platts

Food Stylist
Louise Kenney

Food Stylist Assistants
Jemima Mills
Christina Cullen
Lucy Cottle
Sarah Vassallo

Prop Stylist
Max Robinson

Head of Production
Stephen Lang

Senior Production Controller
Sabeena Atchia

Colour reproduction by F1
Printed in China by C&C Offset Printing Ltd

The authorised representative in the EEA is Penguin Random House Ireland, Morrison Chambers, 32 Nassau Street, Dublin D02 YH68.

Penguin Random House is committed to a sustainable future for our business, our readers and our planet. This book is made from Forest Stewardship Council® certified paper.

CONTENTS

INTRODUCTION

If you've bought this book, you will either have no idea where to start, or will be looking for new ways to use your air fryer. Either way, this book is here to help and I hope you find some recipes you'll enjoy making time and again. Air fryers are much more versatile than their name suggests, enabling you to make almost anything from scratch without too much effort (including things like cakes and stews!).

I really enjoy using my hands and being practical in the kitchen, and you'll see from the recipes throughout these pages that an air fryer can really strengthen your kitchen game. I also wanted to create vegetarian and vegan recipes that don't compromise on flavour or texture. You'll find plenty of salads in this book, along with soups, pasta dishes, a couple of curries and some really good puddings.

For many of these recipes, you will need to do some chopping (which I don't mind) but if you don't have time for this you can always use pre-chopped basic ingredients (usually found in the freezer section at big supermarkets). A couple of the recipes have a little stove-top action (for example, making flatbreads and toasting nuts) because air fryers do have a limit!

If you're looking for a place to start, then the cover photo is of Palestinian Fatteh (page 26), which I urge you to try: it's simple, full of good things and satisfying to eat. It is also a lovely dish to share with others.

A note on ingredients

Most of the recipes use everyday ingredients that you can find in your local shops, markets or supermarkets, and where a recipe needs something unusual (gochujang or cardamom pods, for example), they can be found in a larger supermarket. All the recipes are packed with plants, so by cooking from this book you'll easily be increasing your weekly intake of gut-loving foods!

I instruct to 'crush' your garlic, but I actually prefer to grate mine on a fine Microplane, or small-holed grater. Do try this, as it saves cleaning a garlic crusher – so fiddly!

I use extra virgin olive oil from the bottle when cooking with my air fryer. If you use an oil spray, make sure it is 100% olive oil.

If you want to make some of the recipes when ingredients are out of season locally, then the frozen section of your supermarket can be a brilliant place to find what you are looking for. They are usually a bit cheaper and just need a little time to defrost before cooking. For example, you can use frozen French beans for the roasted bean recipe on page 86, or frozen baby leaf spinach in the West African Peanut Butter Stew or Borek recipes on pages 43 and 107.

Use unwaxed lemons and limes, especially when using the zest. And whenever grated citrus zest appears in a recipe, I mean finely grated; I use a Microplane for this but the fine holes of a box grater are also ideal.

Some reminders about air fryers

Air fryers are fast to heat up (typically they take 3 minutes to reach the desired temperature, as opposed to 10–15 minutes for a conventional oven) and they cook food more quickly, which drastically reduces both your energy consumption and time spent waiting for your dinner!

When air-frying, you need to occasionally turn the food to ensure it cooks evenly – this is easy to do with a wooden spoon or tongs, or simply by giving the basket a gentle shake part-way through cooking.

All the recipes have been developed using a large, single basket-style (5.7-litre/5-quart capacity) air fryer with a removable crisper plate. Once the crisper plate is removed, you can cook on the bottom of the 'basket', which means you can use it a bit like a saucepan or frying pan – this is a really useful function.

Instructions for these types of air fryers are given in each recipe, along with direction on if/when you need to remove the crisper plate. If you have a double-drawer model, then you can cook two recipes simultaneously, or feed larger quantities.

There are so many models around, so if you have an oven-style air fryer or one with a perforated basket, then for some of the recipes you will need to insert a metal or ovenproof dish that fits inside your air fryer and is big enough to hold all the ingredients.

Take care that no food or liquids touch the heating element at the top of your air fryer, as this can cause a fire. Some of the recipes, particularly in the Mains chapter, have a number of ingredients that get cooked together in the air fryer and require you to use your judgement on whether they can all fit in safely or not.

Some air fryers have pre-set function buttons (bake, roast, air-fry, dehydrate and so on) with built-in timers on them, but I find it easiest to set the temperature I want and then adjust the timer. This gives me more accuracy with each recipe.

Do consult the manufacturer's manual to give you some help, as air fryers take some getting used to. As with all appliances, models vary, so you will need to do some experimenting to see what works best for yours.

How an air fryer differs from an oven

Air fryers use convection (just like a conventional oven) to cook food, but the fan is situated at the top of the appliance rather than at the back. The heating element emits air into the cooking chamber while a fan circulates the hot air around it, creating a high-intensity convection oven. The air distribution makes food crisp up, achieving similar results to deep-fat frying. But don't be fooled – you still need to use some oil to ensure perfectly golden food, just not litres of the stuff!

Types and sizes of cooking dishes

You can use the same types of dishes in an air fryer as in an oven; for example cast iron, stainless steel or ovenproof pottery. You can't use plastic, but you can use silicone.

For easy reference, my 5.7-litre (5-quart) basket-style air fryer can fit the following-size dishes inside:

- 20cm (8in) cake tin (pan) that is 9cm (3½in) deep

- 18 × 22cm (7 × 8½in) rectangular baking tin

DOs & DON'Ts

DO preheat your air fryer (this takes about 3 minutes).

DON'T preheat your air fryer with parchment paper inside, or the paper will get sucked up to the heating element and could cause a fire!

DON'T overload your air fryer, otherwise the food won't cook evenly.

DON'T let any liquids, food or fat come into contact with the heating element of your air fryer, or it could break your appliance.

DO be careful when pouring liquids in so they don't splash the heating element (it's best to remove the whole basket or tin/pan and replace it once the liquid has been poured in).

DO use tongs or a spatula to lift food out of the air fryer.

DO use an oven mitt if you have to reach in to remove an item.

DO read the manual of your air fryer, as all models differ.

DO make use of the timer on your air fryer to remind you when to shake the basket/turn food/check if the food is cooked.

DO clean your air fryer in between uses, as the fats can build up.

Essential items

Here is a list of things that are useful to have around when you're using an air fryer; you'll likely have many of these at home already and they will make life much easier when cooking the recipes in this book:

- wooden or silicone-tipped tongs

- traditional or silicone pastry brush

- pre-cut perforated air-fryer parchment liners or a perforated silicone liner

- parchment cake tin (pan) liners

- cake tin that fits inside your air fryer

- roasting tin that fits inside your air fryer

- heatproof trivet or mat

A NOTE ON SYMBOLS

Every recipe is vegetarian, and each tells you if it is also vegan, or can be made vegan. I have given instructions on which recipes suit which type of air fryer and, in most cases, there are also instructions for what to do if you don't have the air fryer type best suited to the recipe. Unless the recipes says to remove the crisper plate, assume it is to be kept in.

VE = vegan

VO = vegan option given

best suited to a basket-style air fryer

best suited to an oven-style air fryer

LIGHT BITES

This chapter is filled with a plethora of salads and soups. Most, if not all, of the salads would work nicely together as part of a buffet, so they are useful recipes if you have people coming over. Soups aren't something you'd ordinarily think about making in an air fryer, but they actually work really well. Most of the soup recipes ask you to air-fry the vegetables first and then you simply use a stick blender or regular blender to blitz in the stock. It's so easy!

VEGETABLE & HALLOUMI TRAYBAKE WITH HERB OIL vo

This is a rustic-looking traybake, perfect for late summer. Super-simple to throw together, and you could add in some crusty bread to soak up the juices. The herb oil adds a finesse to the finished dish, and the warm beans and tomatoes give a sweetness to each bite.

2 courgettes (zucchini),
    roughly chopped
1 red (bell) pepper, deseeded
    and roughly chopped
1 green (bell) pepper, deseeded
    and roughly chopped
1 large red onion, cut into wedges
olive oil, for drizzling
1 × 400g (14oz) can butter beans,
    drained and rinsed
250g (9oz) cherry tomatoes
1 × 250g (9oz) block of halloumi, sliced
    (optional, or use vegan alternative)
sea salt and freshly ground
    black pepper

For the herb oil
small bunch (about 25g/1oz) of basil,
    roughly chopped
small bunch (about 25g/1oz) of dill,
    roughly chopped
3 tbsp extra virgin olive oil
1 tbsp red wine vinegar

Preheat the air fryer to 180°C (350°F), removing the crisper plate.

Add the courgettes (zucchini), (bell) peppers and onion to the air fryer, drizzle with olive oil, season with salt and black pepper, then air-fry for 20 minutes, shaking the basket halfway through cooking. (If you're using an oven-style air fryer or one with a perforated basket, tip everything into a baking tin or cake barrel that fits your air fryer.)

Tip in the beans, give it all a mix, then top with the cherry tomatoes and halloumi slices, if using. Return to the air fryer for 10 minutes.

Meanwhile, make the herb oil. Using a stick blender, blitz all the ingredients together, with salt to taste, until you have a bright green sauce. Add in a little more oil if it's too thick and more salt if needed. You can make this by hand if you prefer: simply finely chop the basil and dill, add to a bowl, then stir in the oil and vinegar, adding salt to taste.

Serve the hot vegetables, making sure everyone has a bit of everything, then drizzle the herb oil over the top.

Serves 4
–
Prep 10 mins
–
Cook 30 mins

ROASTED PEPPER SOUP VO

Developing this recipe was a revelation – it was so easy and delicious – so I really hope you give it a go. It can be served chilled as well as hot, so is a useful recipe to make from the summer through to the autumn. You can use single-colour (bell) peppers or mix it up with a combination of red, yellow, orange and green. All taste delicious, but mixing up the colours will vary the colour of the end result.

1 red onion, thickly sliced
2 garlic cloves, thickly sliced
300g (10½oz) cherry tomatoes
4 (bell) peppers, a mixture of colours if you like, halved and deseeded
4 tbsp extra virgin olive oil
400–500ml (13½–17fl oz/1⅓–2 cups) hot vegetable stock
1½ tbsp pomegranate molasses or balsamic vinegar
sea salt and freshly ground black pepper

To serve
a few chives, finely chopped
sour cream or plain yogurt (optional, or use vegan alternative)

Preheat the air fryer to 180°C (350°F), removing the crisper plate.

Place the onion, garlic and cherry tomatoes in the air fryer, then place the (bell) pepper halves skin side up on top. This will ensure the skins blister and the garlic and onions are protected from the harsh heat. Drizzle over 1 tablespoon of the olive oil, then air-fry for 25 minutes. (If you're using an oven-style air fryer or one with a perforated basket, tip everything into a baking tin or cake barrel that fits your air fryer.)

Transfer everything to a large bowl, add 400ml (13½fl oz/1⅓ cups) of hot stock along with the remaining olive oil and the pomegranate molasses. Season well with salt and black pepper and blitz with a stick blender. Add more stock if you prefer a thinner consistency.

Chill for an hour if you plan to eat this cold. Serve with some chives sprinkled on top, and with a dollop of sour cream if you like.

Serves 4
–
Prep 5 mins
–
Cook 25 mins

ROASTED SWEET POTATO & FETA SALAD

This dish is sweet, salty, crispy and tangy. It works well alongside some of the other salads in this chapter so could be served as part of a buffet. It also sits well and could happily be eaten at room temperature rather than straight out of the air fryer – so consider making it ahead.

5 medium-sized sweet potatoes, washed and unpeeled, cut into wedges
4 banana shallots, peeled and halved lengthways
4½ tbsp olive oil
100g (3½oz) cavolo nero, thickly shredded
1 red chilli, finely chopped
grated zest and juice of 1 lemon
small handful of dill, finely chopped
200g (7oz) feta
sea salt and freshly ground black pepper

Preheat the air fryer to 190°C (375°F).

Mix the sweet potato wedges and banana shallots with 1 tablespoon of the olive oil. Season well with salt, add to the air fryer and air-fry for 20 minutes, shaking the basket halfway through.

Mix the cavolo nero with the chilli and ½ tablespoon of olive oil and add to the sweet potatoes and shallots. Air-fry for another 5 minutes.

Meanwhile, whisk together the remaining 3 tablespoons of olive oil, the lemon zest and juice and dill. Season well with salt and pepper.

Arrange the vegetables on a platter and drizzle over the dressing. Crumble over the feta and serve immediately.

Serves 4
–
Prep 10 mins
–
Cook 25 mins

WARM CAULIFLOWER & GREEN LENTIL SALAD VO

This is another lovely recipe that can be made ahead and is just as good at room temperature as warm. Make sure you don't cut the cauliflower too small, or it will burn – a little larger than bite-sized is ideal, as the pieces reduce in size as they cook.

1 cauliflower, florets cut into large bite-sized pieces, tender leaves reserved
1 tbsp olive oil
400g (14oz) cooked Puy (French) or green lentils, drained
1 tbsp ground cumin
2 tbsp ground coriander
3 garlic cloves, crushed
50g (1¾oz) blanched hazelnuts, roughly chopped
sea salt and freshly ground black pepper

To serve
small bunch of coriander (cilantro), leaves finely chopped
seeds of 1 pomegranate
plain yogurt of choice (or vegan alternative)

Preheat the air fryer to 190°C (375°F), removing the crisper plate.

Mix the cauliflower florets with the olive oil and season well with salt. Add to the air fryer and air-fry for 20 minutes, shaking the basket halfway through cooking and adding the reserved tender leaves for the final 5 minutes. (If you're using an oven-style air fryer or one with a perforated basket, tip the cauliflower into a baking tin or cake barrel that fits your air fryer.)

Mix the lentils with the spices and garlic and season with salt and black pepper. Tip on top of the cauliflower, give it all a good stir and air-fry for another 5 minutes.

Meanwhile, toast the hazelnuts in a dry frying pan for 3–4 minutes, until fragrant and lightly browned.

Serve the cauliflower and lentils warm with the hazelnuts, chopped coriander (cilantro) and pomegranate seeds sprinkled over, and yogurt dolloped on top.

Tip

To remove the seeds from the pomegranate, cut it in half, turn the pomegranate over so that the cut side is sitting against the palm of your hand, then gently tap the bottom with a wooden spoon. The seeds will tumble out through your fingers – make sure you have a bowl sitting underneath to catch them! Remove any white pith before serving.

Serves 4
–
Prep 10 mins
–
Cook 25 mins

PUMPKIN, ORANGE & CUMIN SOUP VE

This is best made on a cold winter's day when you need cheering up. Delica pumpkins are available from autumn through to the early spring: they are harvested in autumn but store well, which is why you can occasionally find them in early spring. The flesh is intensely creamy and rich, so it's worth buying if you can find it. You can use onion squash or Crown Prince if you can't find Delica.

2 garlic cloves, peeled
2 banana shallots, peeled and halved
1 Delica pumpkin (or Crown Prince or onion squash), about 1kg (2lb 4oz), halved and deseeded
1 tbsp ground cumin
drizzle of extra virgin olive oil
500ml (17fl oz/generous 1 cup) hot vegetable stock
juice of 1 orange
hazelnut butter, to serve
sea salt and freshly ground black pepper

Preheat the air fryer to 190°C (375°F).

Divide the garlic and shallots between the pumpkin cavities and sprinkle the cumin over the flesh. Drizzle over a little extra virgin olive oil and sprinkle with salt and black pepper.

Carefully drop the pumpkin halves into the air fryer, cut side down, ensuring the garlic and shallots are enclosed inside the cavity, or they will burn. Air-fry for 35 minutes.

Check the pumpkin is ready by piercing the skin with a sharp knife – if it is tender and cuts easily, it's ready. If not, return to the air fryer for another 5 minutes or so until it's done.

Carefully remove the pumpkin and transfer the garlic and shallots to a heatproof bowl. Using a tea towel to hold the pumpkin (and protect your hands), scoop out the flesh with a spoon and transfer to the bowl. Pour in the hot stock and the orange juice and blitz with a stick blender until smooth. Taste for seasoning, then serve up in bowls with a spoonful of hazelnut butter stirred through.

Serves 4
–
Prep 5 mins
–
Cook 35 mins

WARM SQUASH SALAD

Lovely as a wintry starter or as a light lunch, this is easy to make and is really just arranging good ingredients on a plate. The squash ends up being soft, sweet and a little chewy, then you have the contrast of the crunchy breadcrumbs giving pops of texture. It can look spectacular if you keep the squash slices long so they spill over the side of the plate when served.

1kg (2lb 4oz) butternut squash, skin left on, deseeded and cut into wedges 1cm (½in) thick
3 tbsp extra virgin olive oil
2 rosemary stalks, needles stripped and finely chopped
50g (1¾oz) fresh breadcrumbs
small bunch of flat-leaf parsley, leaves finely chopped
1 garlic clove, crushed
25g (1oz) Parmesan, finely grated, plus extra to serve
60g (2¼oz) rocket (arugula)
juice of 1 lemon
sea salt and freshly ground black pepper

Preheat the air fryer to 190°C (375°F).

Mix the squash chunks with 2 tablespoons of the olive oil, some salt and pepper, and the chopped rosemary. Tip into the air fryer and roast for 30 minutes until the flesh is tender and the skin is slightly blistered and blackened in places, giving the basket a shake halfway through.

Meanwhile, mix the breadcrumbs with the parsley, garlic, grated parmesan and remaining tablespoon of olive oil. Once the squash has had its time, sprinkle over the breadcrumb mixture and return to the air fryer for 5 more minutes.

Remove and set aside to cool briefly.

When you are ready to serve, arrange the rocket (arugula) on a platter and tumble the squash over the top. Drizzle over the lemon juice and shave or grate over some extra Parmesan.

Serves 4
–
Prep 15 mins
–
Cook 35 mins

CELERIAC, PARSNIP & APPLE SOUP VE

Sweet and aniseedy in flavour, celeriac (celery root) is the ugly duckling of vegetables. It should not be judged by its appearance however, but by the depth of flavour it brings to any number of dishes. Here it's paired with sweet parsnip and apple to give a satisfying autumnal soup.

500g (1lb 2oz) celeriac (celery root), peeled and cut into 2cm (¾in) pieces
200g (7oz) parsnips (about 2 small parsnips), peeled and cut into 2cm (¾in) pieces
1 onion, roughly chopped
2 Granny Smith apples, peeled, cored and quartered
olive oil, for drizzling
1.25 litres (42fl oz/5¼ cups) hot vegetable stock
2 tbsp hazelnut or almond butter (optional)
small bunch of flat-leaf parsley, leaves roughly chopped, to serve
sea salt and freshly ground black pepper

Preheat the air fryer to 190°C (375°F).

Tip the vegetables and apples into the air fryer, season with salt and pepper and drizzle with a little olive oil. Roast for 30 minutes, stirring a couple of times during cooking, until nice and tender with some caramelization around the edges.

Tip the vegetables into a blender, or a bowl, pour in the hot stock and the nut butter (if using) and blitz until smooth. Check the consistency is how you like it and add more stock or hot water if you prefer a thinner soup. Taste for seasoning and serve immediately, with parsley sprinkled on top, in warm bowls.

Serves 6–8
–
Prep 10 mins
–
Cook 30 mins

PALESTINIAN FATTEH VO

What a gem of a recipe this is. Using simple ingredients with well-known flavour combinations, it nonetheless never fails to delight both in texture and appearance. I hope you enjoy making it as much as I do.

6 pitta breads, cut or torn into pieces
2 tbsp olive oil
1 tsp ground cumin
juice of 1 lemon
3 garlic cloves, crushed
handful of flat-leaf parsley leaves, roughly chopped
2 tbsp tahini
200g (7oz) plain yogurt (or vegan alternative)
2 × 400g (14oz) cans chickpeas (garbanzos), drained and rinsed
50g (1¾oz) pine nuts
sea salt and freshly ground black pepper

To serve
seeds of 1 pomegranate
large handful of rocket (arugula)

Preheat the air fryer to 190°C (375°F), removing the crisper plate.

Mix the pitta pieces with the olive oil and season with salt, then tip into the air fryer and air-fry for 9 minutes, shaking the basket halfway through.

Meanwhile, make the sauce, either using a food processor or a stick blender. Blitz together the cumin, lemon juice, garlic, parsley, tahini, yogurt and half the chickpeas (garbanzos) until you have a thick sauce. Season with salt and pepper.

Remove the pitta from the air fryer and add the remaining chickpeas and the pine nuts. Air-fry for 8 minutes until they are warmed through and beginning to colour.

To assemble the salad, scatter the crispy pitta over a platter, pour over the sauce, then top with the warm chickpeas and pine nuts. Finally, scatter over the pomegranate seeds and rocket (arugula).

Serve immediately while the pitta is still crisp.

Serves 4
–
Prep 10 mins
–
Cook 17 mins

CABBAGE & CORIANDER SOUP VE

This soup is best made in the bottom of the air-fryer basket, so if you have an oven-style one or a perforated basket, this recipe won't work so well. You will need to have at least a 5-litre (4½-quart) air fryer, which will accommodate all the ingredients, as it's important not to let any liquid splash the heating element.

1 tbsp extra virgin olive oil
1 onion, finely chopped
2 garlic cloves, crushed
5cm (2in) piece of fresh root ginger, finely grated
1 green chilli, deseeded and finely chopped
400g (14oz) Savoy cabbage or cavolo nero, finely shredded
1 tbsp ground coriander
800ml (27fl oz/3¹/₃ cups) hot vegetable stock
1 × 400g (14oz) can coconut milk
grated zest and juice of 2 limes
small bunch of coriander (cilantro), leaves finely chopped, to serve
sea salt and freshly ground black pepper

Preheat the air fryer to 190°C (375°F), removing the crisper plate.

Mix the olive oil with the onion, garlic, ginger, chilli, cabbage and ground coriander. Tip everything into the base of the air-fryer basket and cook for 5 minutes, stirring halfway through.

Carefully pour in the hot stock and coconut milk, then season with salt and pepper. Cook for another 7 minutes, stirring a few times.

Finally, stir in the lime zest and juice. Taste and season with salt and pepper if needed, then serve with a sprinkle of chopped coriander (cilantro).

Serves 4
–
Prep 10 mins
–
Cook 12 mins

SPICED BEETROOT WITH LENTILS & GOAT'S CHEESE

I took my inspiration for this salad from *Sarah Raven's Garden Cookbook*, adapting it for the air fryer. I like to mix this with my hands, thereby ensuring the ingredients are properly combined, but if you prefer not to get beetroot-stained skin then use salad servers. The spices get toasted then ground up at the start, so you'll need either a spice/coffee grinder or pestle and mortar for the job.

1 tbsp cumin seeds
1 tbsp coriander seeds
1 tbsp fennel seeds
8 whole raw beetroot (beet), the size of small lemons, peeled and cut into 3cm (1¼in) chunks
2 tsp sea salt
3 tbsp extra virgin olive oil
250g (9oz) cooked Beluga lentils
small bunch of mint, leaves finely chopped
small bunch of flat-leaf parsley, leaves finely chopped
bunch of watercress, roughly chopped
handful of cherry tomatoes, quartered
1 red chilli, finely chopped (optional)
grated zest and juice of 1 lemon
250g (9oz) fresh goat's cheese
ciabatta, to serve

Preheat the air fryer to 190°C (375°F), removing the crisper plate.

Dry-fry (no oil needed!) the cumin, coriander and fennel seeds in a frying pan set over a high heat for a couple of minutes until fragrant and toasted. Tip into a pestle and mortar (or use a spice/coffee grinder) and crush until finely ground.

Mix the beetroot (beet) with the ground spices, salt and 1 tablespoon of the olive oil, then tip into the air fryer and roast for 35 minutes until tender. Remove to a bowl and set aside to cool for a few minutes.

In a large salad bowl, mix together the lentils, mint, parsley, watercress, tomatoes and chilli, if using. Add the spiced beetroot and mix again.

Stir the remaining 2 tablespoons of olive oil with the lemon zest and juice, and pour over the salad. Leave to sit for 10 minutes, to allow the flavours to combine.

Finally, dot over the fresh goat's cheese and serve with some warm ciabatta.

Serves 4
–
Prep 20 mins
–
Cook 35 mins

Light Bites

ROASTED COURGETTE, AUBERGINE & RED ONION SALAD VO

A lovely, fresh lunchtime salad. This was inspired by tabbouleh, hence the herbs and grains, and it would work well as part of a number of salads for a buffet-style meal.

150g (5½oz) bulgur wheat
1 aubergine (eggplant), cut into 1–2cm (½–¾in) chunks
2 medium courgettes (zucchini), cut into 1–2cm (½–¾in) chunks
1 red onion, thickly sliced
2 tbsp olive oil
1 garlic clove, finely sliced
100g (3½oz) curly kale, stalks removed and leaves torn into 1cm (½in) pieces
grated zest of 2 oranges and flesh roughly chopped
small bunch of mint, leaves finely chopped
small bunch of flat-leaf parsley, leaves finely chopped
sea salt and freshly ground black pepper

To serve
drizzle of sherry vinegar
Greek yogurt (optional, or use vegan alternative)

Preheat the air fryer to 190°C (375°F).

Put the bulgur wheat in a heatproof bowl and add enough boiling water to just submerge the grains, then season well with salt and pepper. Cover the bowl with a plate and leave to steam while the vegetables cook. It will suck up all the water and the grains will plump up.

Mix the aubergine (eggplant), courgette (zucchini) and onion with the olive oil and season well with salt and pepper.

Tip the veg into the air fryer and roast for 20 minutes, stirring a couple of times during cooking. Stir in the garlic and kale and air-fry for another 5 minutes.

Mix the orange zest, flesh and herbs together, then stir in the cooked vegetables and soaked bulgur wheat, which should have absorbed the water by now. If not, drain off any excess water and then add the grains to the rest of the salad ingredients.

Arrange everything in a wide bowl, drizzle over some sherry vinegar and dollop on a few spoonfuls of Greek yogurt (if using).

Serves 4
–
Prep 15 mins
–
Cook 25 mins

Light Bites

MAINS

If you want to try something super speedy right away, then head to page 40 for the Singapore Noodles, or page 54 for the Courgette, Dill & Lemon Farfalle. Heartier dishes (that really make your air fryer work hard) can be found on page 43 for West African Peanut Butter Stew or page 63 for Veggie Crumble.

MUSHROOM & WALNUT RAGÙ VO

This is packed with good things – you could add in cooked green lentils in place of the cauliflower for extra protein. Using a food processor will save time and elbow grease, but you can do this by hand if you prefer to do things slowly. Tagliatelle or pappardelle are ideal for this ragù.

You will need to have at least a 5-litre (4½-quart) air fryer which will accommodate all the ingredients, as it's important not to let any liquid splash the heating element.

1 celery stick
1 leek, washed
1 carrot, peeled
250g (9oz) chestnut (cremini) mushrooms
3 garlic cloves
1 small cauliflower, leaves removed
100g (3½oz) walnuts
50g (1¾oz) cooked chestnuts
6 sprigs of thyme, leaves picked
olive oil, for drizzling
1 tbsp brown rice miso paste
4 tbsp tomato purée (paste)
1 × 400g (14oz) can chopped tomatoes
350ml (12fl oz/1½ cups) hot vegetable stock
1 bay leaf
sea salt and freshly ground black pepper

To serve
your choice of cooked long pasta
grated Parmesan (optional, or use vegan alternative)

If using a food processor to chop the vegetables, roughly chop the celery, leek, carrot, mushrooms and garlic by hand, then finely chop in a food processor – take care not to over-process them or everything will go mushy. Remove to a bowl and repeat the process with the cauliflower, walnuts and chestnuts. If chopping by hand, finely chop all the vegetables and nuts.

Preheat the air fryer to 190°C (375°F), removing the crisper plate.

Mix all the veggies and nuts together along with the thyme leaves. Spoon onto the base of your air-fryer basket. Season well with salt and pepper and drizzle with olive oil. Air-fry for 20 minutes, stirring 2 or 3 times during cooking.

Whisk together the miso, tomato purée (paste), chopped tomatoes and vegetable stock. Pour this over the vegetables and mix well. Tuck in the bay leaf and return to the air fryer for another 15 minutes.

Taste and check the seasoning, adding more salt and pepper if you need it. Serve over your choice of cooked long pasta, with Parmesan grated over the top if you like.

Serves 6
–
Prep 20 mins
–
Cook 35 mins

AUBERGINE & PARMESAN BAKE

Silky-soft aubergine (eggplant) shrouded in a sweet tomato sauce and plenty of melted mozzarella, this is based on the popular melanzane parmigiana and makes a great lunch for two with a crisp salad of radicchio and bitter green leaves on the side. You need a cake barrel or an ovenproof dish that fits your air fryer. I used one that was 18 × 22cm (7 × 8¾in).

2 aubergines (eggplants), cut into 5mm (¼in) discs
1 onion, finely chopped
2 garlic cloves, crushed
4 tbsp olive oil
1 × 400g (14oz) can finely chopped tomatoes
small bunch of basil, leaves finely chopped
1 × 150g (5½oz) ball of mozzarella, drained
50g (1¾oz) Parmesan, finely grated
radicchio and bitter green leaves, to serve
sea salt and freshly ground black pepper

For the wholegrain mustard vinaigrette
6 tbsp olive oil
2 tbsp red wine vinegar
1 tsp wholegrain mustard

Lay the aubergine (eggplant) slices in a colander, sprinkling each layer generously with salt. Set over a bowl or in the sink so the juices can drain while you carry on with the recipe.

Preheat the air fryer to 180°C (350°F).

Put the onion and garlic in a cake barrel or ovenproof dish that will fit inside your air fryer, drizzle with 1 tablespoon of the olive oil and season with salt and pepper. Air-fry for 10 minutes, stirring halfway through. Pour in the tomatoes, half a can of water, the basil and some salt and pepper. Stir and air-fry for 10 more minutes, then remove and set aside.

Turn up the air fryer to 200°C (400°F).

Rinse the aubergines and pat dry. Mix them with the remaining 3 tablespoons of olive oil, making sure each slice is coated. Pop the slices into the air fryer in as even a layer as possible, but don't worry if some slices are overlapping. Air-fry for 20 minutes, turning the slices halfway through to ensure they all cook evenly.

Spread a third of the tomato sauce over the bottom of your ovenproof dish. Layer half the aubergines on top, tear over half the mozzarella, then sprinkle over half the Parmesan. Repeat with a second layer of tomato sauce, then the remaining aubergines. Spread over the final third of tomato sauce and top with the remaining mozzarella and Parmesan. Air-fry for 8 minutes until golden and bubbling.

Meanwhile, to make the vinaigrette, put all the dressing ingredients into a jar and give it a good shake. Drizzle over the salad leaves and serve alongside the aubergine bake.

Serves 2 for lunch or 4 as a side
–
Prep 20 mins
–
Cook 45 mins

SINGAPORE NOODLES VE

You don't need a wok to make these noodles – the air fryer does all the work for you and they are a cinch to make. All that is required is some initial chopping and then you are good to go. I'd recommend getting everything prepared before you start up your air fryer, as this will save you time.

1 tbsp toasted sesame oil
1 thumb-sized piece of fresh root
    ginger, peeled and finely chopped
3 spring onions (scallions), finely sliced
1 red (bell) pepper, deseeded and
    finely sliced
1 large carrot, peeled and cut
    into matchsticks
½ small Savoy cabbage, finely sliced
200g (7oz) ready-cooked
    vermicelli noodles
200g (7oz) bean sprouts, washed
3 tbsp soy sauce
1½ tbsp mild curry powder
1 tsp Shaoxing rice wine
½ tbsp black sesame seeds
coriander (cilantro) leaves, to serve
sea salt and freshly ground
    black pepper

Preheat the air fryer to 190°C (375°F), removing the crisper plate.

Pour ½ tablespoon of the sesame oil into the base of your air-fryer basket, then add the ginger, spring onions (scallions), red (bell) pepper, carrot and cabbage. Season with salt and pepper, give it a good mix and air-fry for 10 minutes. (If you're using an oven-style air fryer or one with a perforated basket, tip everything into a baking tin or cake barrel that fits your air fryer.)

Add the noodles, bean sprouts, soy sauce, curry powder, rice wine, remaining sesame oil and the sesame seeds and give it all a good mix. Return to the air fryer for 3 more minutes.

Remove and serve in warm noodle bowls with some coriander (cilantro) sprinkled over the top.

Serves 2
–
Prep 10 mins
–
Cook 13 mins

WEST AFRICAN PEANUT BUTTER STEW VE

I had a variation of this as a soup in a café a few years ago. It was so delicious that I made a mental note to come up with my own version. Rich, creamy and spicy, this is sure to fill you up, and there are so many plants in here, you can feel virtuous at the same time! It takes some preparation but is worth it. You could use fresh instead of frozen spinach, but you'll need to wilt it first before adding to the air fryer.

You will need at least a 5-litre (4½-quart) air fryer to accommodate all the ingredients, as it's important not to let any liquid splash the heating element.

For the spice base
2 tbsp sunflower oil
1 onion, roughly chopped
4 garlic cloves, roughly chopped
large thumb-sized piece of fresh root
    ginger, peeled and roughly chopped
1 tsp chilli (red pepper) flakes
2 tsp ground coriander
1 tsp ground turmeric
2 tsp ground cumin
2 tbsp tomato purée (paste)

For the stew
1 small (500g/1lb 2oz) butternut
    squash, peeled, deseeded and cut
    into 0.5–1cm (¼–½in) chunks
250g (9oz) crunchy peanut butter
400g (14oz) passata (puréed
    strained tomatoes)
400ml (13½fl oz/1⅔ cups) hot
    vegetable stock
pinch of sugar
1 × 400g (14oz) can black beans
150g (5½oz) frozen baby leaf spinach
sea salt and freshly ground
    black pepper

To serve
juice of 1 or 2 limes
handful of salted peanuts,
    roughly chopped
3 spring onions (scallions), finely sliced
small bunch of coriander (cilantro),
    leaves roughly chopped
1 red chilli, finely chopped
flatbreads (see page 114 for
    homemade) or cooked brown rice
plain yogurt (optional, or use
    vegan alternative)

Preheat the air fryer to 180°C (350°F), removing the crisper plate.

In a food processor or blender, blend together the spice-base ingredients until they make a paste. Use a splash of water to loosen if necessary.

Mix the butternut squash with the spice paste, season with salt and pepper and add to the base of your air-fryer basket. Roast for 40 minutes, stirring a few times during cooking and adding a splash of water if it gets too dry.

Mix together the peanut butter, passata (strained tomatoes), stock and sugar, and pour this into the air fryer. Add the black beans, along with the liquid from the can, season again with salt and give it all a good mix. Air-fry for 30 minutes, stirring halfway through, then stir in the frozen spinach and air-fry for another 5 minutes, until the spinach has defrosted and the vegetables are tender.

Transfer to bowls and squeeze over some lime juice. Top with chopped peanuts, spring onions (scallions), fresh coriander (cilantro) and chilli, and serve with flatbreads or brown rice, or on its own, with a spoonful of yogurt dolloped on top.

Serves 6
–
Prep 30 mins
–
Cook 75 mins

Mains

GREEN PASTA

A super-speedy, low-prep pasta dish. This sauce goes down well with children, if they like broccoli! Otherwise, keep this for the grown-ups.

3 tbsp extra virgin olive oil
3 garlic cloves, finely sliced
400g (14oz) tenderstem or purple sprouting broccoli, finely chopped
350g (12½oz) linguine, spaghetti or other long pasta
grated zest and juice of 1 lemon
50g (1¾oz) Parmesan, freshly grated, plus extra to serve
handful of flat-leaf parsley leaves, finely chopped
1 red chilli, finely chopped (optional)
sea salt and freshly ground black pepper

Preheat the air fryer to 190°C (375°F), removing the crisper plate.

Add the olive oil and garlic slices to the base of your air-fryer basket and air-fry for 2–3 minutes. Tip the broccoli into the air fryer, mix well and air-fry for another 7 minutes, until crispy and charred in places.

Meanwhile, cook the pasta in a pan of boiling, salted water, according to the packet instructions, then drain and reserve a ladleful or two of the cooking water.

Mix the cooked pasta with the garlicky broccoli, stir in the lemon zest and juice, Parmesan and parsley and check the seasoning. Add a spoonful or two of the pasta cooking water if it all looks too dry. Sprinkle over the chilli, if using, and divide between warm bowls.

Grate over more Parmesan to serve.

Serves 4
–
Prep 5 mins
–
Cook 10 mins

THREE BEAN STEW VO

A hearty stew goes so well with anything, from baked potatoes and cheese to toasted pitta and a fried egg. You can use any variety of cooked, canned beans here – just make sure there is a mixture of shapes and colours. If you can get hold of cans of finely chopped tomatoes, all the better, but the ordinary sort is fine too. If you're using a cake barrel to cook this, then make sure none of the ingredients touch or splash onto the heating element once they are all in.

2 celery sticks, finely sliced
1 large carrot, peeled and
    finely chopped
1 leek, washed and finely chopped
1 tbsp extra virgin olive oil
1 × 400g (14oz) can borlotti beans,
    drained and rinsed
1 × 400g (14oz) can cannellini beans,
    drained and rinsed
1 × 400g (14oz) can black beans,
    drained and rinsed
2 × 400g (14oz) cans chopped
    tomatoes
2 tbsp tomato purée (paste)
2 sprigs of rosemary, needles
    finely chopped
small bunch of flat-leaf parsley,
    leaves finely chopped
1 bay leaf
handful of pitted marinated
    black olives
sea salt and freshly ground
    black pepper

To serve
grated Cheddar (optional, or use
    vegan alternative)
sour cream (optional, or use
    vegan alternative)

Preheat the air fryer to 180°C (350°F), removing the crisper plate.

Mix the celery, carrot and leek with the olive oil and season with salt and pepper. Tip onto the base of the air-fryer basket and cook for 10 minutes, stirring halfway through. (If you're using an oven-style air fryer or one with a perforated basket, tip everything into a baking tin or cake barrel that fits your air fryer.)

Tip in the drained beans, chopped tomatoes, tomato purée (paste), chopped rosemary and parsley, the bay leaf and black olives. Fill one of the tomato cans with water and add this too. Season well again, then give it all a good stir and return to cook for another 30 minutes, stirring 2 or 3 times during cooking.

Serve in bowls with grated cheese and/or a dollop of sour cream, if you like.

Serves 4
–
Prep 10 mins
–
Cook 40 mins

BORLOTTI BEAN RATATOUILLE VO

I love a ratatouille. Although this is not a traditional recipe, it is still delicious. You could serve it with a crispy fried egg on top, or you could also enjoy it with some French bread. The aubergine (eggplant) flesh melts down in the air fryer and the skin goes a little chewy. If you're using a cake barrel to cook this, make sure none of the ingredients touch or splash onto the heating element once they are all in.

1 onion, thickly sliced
1 large aubergine (eggplant), cut into
    1cm (½in) chunks
1 courgette (zucchini), cut into 1cm
    (½in) chunks
2 tbsp olive oil
1 × 400g (14oz) can borlotti beans,
    drained and rinsed
1 garlic clove, crushed
2 tbsp tomato purée (paste)
1 × 400g (14oz) can chopped tomatoes
small bunch of basil, leaves
    finely chopped
1 tbsp balsamic vinegar
fried eggs, to serve (optional)
sea salt and freshly ground
    black pepper

Preheat the air fryer to 180°C (350°F), removing the crisper plate.

Mix the onion, aubergine (eggplant) and courgette (zucchini) together with the olive oil and some salt and pepper. Tip into the air fryer and roast for 20 minutes, shaking the basket halfway through. (If you're using an oven-style air fryer or one with a perforated basket, tip everything into a baking tin or cake barrel that fits your air fryer.)

Meanwhile, mix together the borlotti beans, garlic, tomato purée (paste) and canned tomatoes. Half fill the empty tomato can and add this too.

Once the vegetables are tender, pour in the tomato and bean mixture, then season with salt and pepper and cook for another 20 minutes.

Finally, stir through the basil and balsamic vinegar and serve immediately, topped with a fried egg if you like.

Serves 4
–
Prep 15 mins
–
Cook 40 mins

Mains

49

ORZO PUTTANESCA VE

A mix between a risotto and a pasta dish, this is one-pot cooking in an air fryer. Little ones will enjoy orzo or the mini star-shaped pasta usually reserved for soups. Just omit the chilli and anything that resembles a vegetable... or perhaps that's just my children? This recipe works best in a wide (non-perforated) basket-style air fryer; if you have a smaller one, reduce the recipe by half.

2 tbsp olive oil
1 onion, finely chopped
2 garlic cloves, crushed
1 tbsp capers
1 tsp chilli (red pepper) flakes
2 × 400g (14oz) cans finely
   chopped tomatoes
½ tbsp white miso paste
100g (3½oz) pitted Kalamata olives
300g (10½oz) orzo or stellette/
   stelline pasta
small bunch of flat-leaf parsley,
   leaves finely chopped
sea salt and freshly ground
   black pepper

Preheat the air fryer to 180°C (350°F), removing the crisper plate.

Add 1 tablespoon of the oil to the base of the air-fryer basket. Tip in the onion and air-fry for 10 minutes, stirring halfway through.

Add the remaining oil with the remaining ingredients, except the parsley, giving it a good stir. Boil a kettle and fill one empty tomato can with boiling water, then half-fill the second can and carefully pour all the water into the air fryer. Season well with salt and pepper.

Cook for a further 35 minutes, stirring a few times during cooking. Leave to stand in the air fryer for 10 minutes, then stir in the parsley and serve.

Serves 4
–
Prep 5 mins
–
Cook 45 mins
–
Rest 10 mins

Mains

TOMATO & MASCARPONE PASTA

At university, my Italian friend, Will, would come over with dried pasta, a can of tomatoes and some mascarpone and he'd make lunch for my friend Bryony and me. I had never tasted anything like it and I've been making it ever since. My kids really enjoy eating this, especially if they get to choose the pasta shape.

800g (1lb 12oz) cherry tomatoes
2 garlic cloves, finely sliced
1 tbsp olive oil
350g (12½oz) conchiglie rigate pasta
    (or short pasta of choice)
3 tbsp mascarpone cheese
small bunch of basil, leaves
    finely chopped
grated Parmesan, to serve (optional)
sea salt and freshly ground
    black pepper

Preheat the air fryer to 190°C (375°F), removing the crisper plate.

Place the tomatoes, garlic, olive oil and some salt and pepper on the base of the air-fryer basket, mix briefly, then cook for 10 minutes. (If you're using an oven-style air fryer or one with a perforated basket, tip everything into a baking tin or cake barrel that fits your air fryer.)

Meanwhile, cook the pasta in a pan of boiling, salted water, according to the packet instructions, then drain and return to the pan.

Tip the tomatoes and any cooking juices onto the drained pasta, then add the mascarpone and basil. Stir well and serve immediately, with some freshly grated Parmesan over the top, if you like.

Serves 4
–
Prep 2 mins
–
Cook 10 mins

COURGETTE, DILL & LEMON FARFALLE VE

A bright, late-summer dish that takes about 15 minutes from first chop to eating! The lemon slices cook down so the skin softens and the juice naturally disperses, leaving you with a really zingy pasta dish – try to slice the lemon as finely as you can to help the slices cook down in the time.

350g (12½oz) farfalle pasta
2 large courgettes (zucchini), finely sliced
1 unwaxed lemon, finely sliced
1 tbsp extra virgin olive oil
1 tbsp nonpareil salted capers, rinsed to remove the salt
50g (1¾oz) pine nuts
small bunch of dill, finely chopped
sea salt and freshly ground black pepper

Preheat the air fryer to 200°C (400°F), removing the crisper plate.

Cook the pasta in a pan of boiling, salted water, according to the packet instructions, then drain and set aside. You can do this while the courgettes (zucchini) cook, to keep everything hot.

Mix the courgette (zucchini) and lemon slices with the olive oil and season well with salt and pepper. Tip onto the base of the air-fryer basket and cook for 10 minutes, stirring halfway through. (If you're using an oven-style air fryer or one with a perforated basket, use a baking tin or cake barrel that fits your air fryer.)

Add the capers and stir well, then sprinkle over the pine nuts and air-fry for another 5 minutes.

Mix the courgettes with the drained pasta and stir through the dill. Serve immediately in warmed pasta bowls.

Serves 4
–
Prep 5 mins
–
Cook 15 mins

VEGETABLE KORMA VO

A gently golden curry with a tiny kick from the green chilli. If you make the flatbreads, this becomes a complete meal – the bread will sit happily for half an hour under a clean tea towel, so you can make them before you prepare the curry if you like. I like to feel efficient so I tend to make the breads while the vegetables are cooking.

You will need at least a 5-litre (4½-quart) air fryer to accommodate all the ingredients, as it's important not to let any liquid splash the heating element.

1 red onion, finely chopped
½ small cauliflower (about 300g/10½oz), cut into bite-sized pieces
1 aubergine (eggplant), roughly chopped
2 small baking potatoes, peeled and cut into 1cm (½in) pieces
1 green chilli, deseeded and finely chopped
2 garlic cloves, crushed
5cm (2in) piece of fresh root ginger, finely grated
2 tbsp ground almonds
seeds of 3 cardamom pods, crushed
2 tsp each of ground cumin and coriander
½ tsp ground turmeric
3 tbsp olive oil
200g (7oz) frozen spinach
300ml (10½fl oz/1¼ cups) hot vegetable stock
200ml (7fl oz/scant 1 cup) double (heavy) cream (or vegan alternative)
sea salt and freshly ground black pepper

For the flatbreads (optional)
200g (7oz) plain yogurt (or vegan alternative)
200g (7oz) self-raising flour, plus extra for dusting
1 tsp extra virgin olive oil

Preheat the air fryer to 180°C (350°F), removing the crisper plate.

Mix the onion, cauliflower, aubergine (eggplant), potatoes, chilli, garlic, ginger, ground almonds and spices with the olive oil and some salt and pepper to taste. Tip the whole lot onto the base of the air-fryer basket and cook for 20 minutes until everything is just tender, stirring halfway through.

Stir in the frozen spinach and hot stock and cook for a further 10 minutes. Finally, pour in the cream and cook for another 3 minutes.

Meanwhile, if you are making flatbreads, in a bowl mix together the yogurt, flour and oil to form a soft dough. Tip out onto a lightly floured surface and knead for 5 minutes until smooth, then rest for 15 minutes to allow the dough to relax (so you can roll them out more easily). Separate the dough into 4 balls, then roll each into a teardrop shape on a lightly floured surface. Heat a frying pan until really hot, then dry-fry (no oil required) on each side until blackened in places and puffed up. Keep warm until you are ready to serve.

Serve the korma in deep bowls with the flatbreads alongside.

Serves 4
–
Prep 20 mins
–
Cook 33 mins

BLACK BEAN BURGERS VE

If you squint, these look like beef burgers. No, I'm kidding – but they do look yummy! They are soft and really juicy, which makes them delicious to eat, but you need to take care when turning them, so they don't break apart. I like to use a stepped palette knife but a fish slice or metal spatula will also work well. These are excellent served with the Piri Piri Fries on page 84.

For the burgers
1 onion, finely chopped
1 carrot, peeled and coarsely grated
2 × 400g (14oz) cans black beans, drained and rinsed
1 tsp piri piri seasoning
1 tsp dried Italian herbs
2 tbsp flaxseed
2 tbsp extra virgin olive oil
1 tbsp soy sauce
1 tbsp balsamic vinegar
50g (1¾oz) panko breadcrumbs
small bunch of flat-leaf parsley, leaves finely chopped
sea salt and freshly ground black pepper

To serve
4 burger buns
a few lettuce leaves
1 small red onion, thinly sliced into rings
2 tomatoes, sliced
a few gherkins, sliced
vegan mayonnaise
tomato ketchup

Mix all the burger ingredients together, with salt and pepper to taste, and mash slightly with a potato masher – you want to break up some of the black beans so the patties hold together. Shape into 4 patties and leave to rest for 10 minutes to firm up.

Preheat the air fryer to 190°C (375°F). Air-fry the burgers for 22 minutes, carefully turning them after 15 minutes to cook the other side.

Serve in burger buns, with all the other things that make a burger delicious! Don't be shy – go big or go home!

Serves 4
–
Prep 20 mins
–
Cook 22 mins

SPINACH & RICOTTA CANNELLONI

Can you cook pasta in an air fryer? Yes you can! This recipe really just needs assembling and the air fryer does the rest. You'll need a deep tin (pan) that fits your air fryer: I used one that was 22 × 18 × 6cm (8¾ x 7 × 2½in). It is best cooked on the crisper plate so the air circulates around the tin. Ensure you use fresh lasagne sheets so that you can roll the filling in the pasta.

300g (10½oz) baby leaf spinach
250g (9oz) ricotta
50g (1¾oz) Parmesan, grated
fresh grating of nutmeg
5–6 fresh lasagne sheets
    (about 200g/7oz)
1 × 150g (5½oz) ball of mozzarella,
    drained
sea salt and freshly ground
    black pepper

For the sauce
350g (12½oz) passata (puréed
    strained tomatoes)
1 tsp dried Italian herbs
2 garlic cloves, crushed
2 tbsp olive oil
1 tbsp red wine vinegar
small bunch of basil, leaves
    finely chopped

In a heatproof bowl, cover the spinach with boiling water and set aside for 5 minutes. Drain, squeeze as much of the water out as you can, then finely chop.

In a bowl, mix the chopped spinach with the ricotta, Parmesan, a few gratings of nutmeg and some salt and pepper to taste. Set aside.

Whisk together the sauce ingredients until well combined, with salt and pepper to taste, then spread two-thirds of the sauce over the bottom of a baking tin (pan) that fits in your air fryer.

Trim the edges of the lasagne sheets so they fit snugly in a row inside the tin once rolled up.

Spoon some of the ricotta mixture along the short edge of a lasagne sheet, then roll it up to make a fat tube. Place seam side down on the tomato sauce and repeat this process until all the sheets and filling have been used up.

Preheat the air fryer to 170°C (340°F).

Spoon the remaining sauce over the top and in between each tube, then tear the mozzarella and dot over the top. Air-fry for 25 minutes until the sauce is bubbling and the cheese has browned on top.

Serve with a crisp green salad on the side.

Serves 2
–
Prep 25 mins
–
Cook 25 mins

VEGGIE CRUMBLE

My husband and I ate this for two suppers on the trot and it was just as good reheated on the second day. The filling is rich and creamy and I've given you a cheat's method for a béchamel – no cooking on the hob; just whisk it together and bung it in the air fryer to thicken up. Genius! I bake this in a 9cm (3½in) deep cake barrel but you could use a shallower receptacle; just make sure you can fit all of the ingredients inside.

For the filling
2 leeks, washed and sliced 1cm (½in) thick
300g (10½oz) celeriac (celery root), peeled and cut into 1cm (½in) chunks
300g (10½oz) sweet potato, peeled and cut into 1cm (½in) chunks
2 tbsp olive oil
450ml (15fl oz/scant 2 cups) whole milk
1 tbsp wholegrain mustard
1 garlic clove, crushed
50g (1¾oz) unsalted butter, melted
50g (1¾oz) plain (all-purpose) flour
50g (1¾oz) Cheddar, grated
sea salt and freshly ground black pepper

For the crumble topping
30g (1oz) jumbo oats
3 tbsp mixed seeds
100g (3½oz) plain (all-purpose) flour
50g (1¾oz) cold unsalted butter, cubed
80g (2¾oz) Cheddar, grated
sea salt and freshly ground black pepper

Preheat the air fryer to 180°C (350°F), removing the crisper plate.

In a bowl, mix the leeks, celeriac (celery root) and sweet potato with the olive oil and season well with salt and pepper. Place in the air fryer and roast for 25 minutes until everything is tender and browned at the edges, stirring a couple of times during cooking. (If you're using an oven-style air fryer or one with a perforated basket, use a baking tin or cake barrel that fits your air fryer.)

Whisk the milk together with the mustard, garlic, melted butter and flour until combined, then stir in the Cheddar. Season with a little salt and pepper.

Once the vegetables have had their cooking time, pour over the milk mixture and return to the air fryer for 10 minutes. The sauce should thicken up nicely around the vegetables. Transfer everything to a cake barrel or similar tin (pan), and set aside. Give your air fryer a quick clean and put the crisper plate inside.

For the crumble topping, mix the oats, seeds and flour together in a bowl. Rub the butter in with your fingertips until you have a sandy texture, then stir in the Cheddar. Season with a little salt and pepper, then sprinkle the mixture over the top of the creamy vegetables.

Reheat the air fryer to 180°C (350°F) and bake the crumble for 15 minutes until golden on top and the sauce is bubbling.

Serves 4
–
Prep 30 mins
–
Cook 50 mins

FILO
PIE VE

A mixture of oyster, shiitake and chestnut (cremini) mushrooms works well here. I baked this in an 8cm (3in) deep cast-iron pot and brought it to the table looking golden and delicious. If you are using an oven-style air fryer you'll need to cook the mushrooms and spinach in a suitable tin. This makes a good Valentine's meal, but only if you like sharing!

500g (1lb 2oz) mixed mushrooms, brushed clean of any dirt, then sliced or torn into chunks
2 garlic cloves, crushed
5 tbsp olive oil
200g (7oz) frozen baby leaf spinach
180g (6½oz) cooked chestnuts, crumbled
30g (1oz) plain (all-purpose) flour
250ml (8½fl oz/1 cup) unsweetened soy milk
1 tsp brown rice miso paste
1 tbsp Dijon mustard
small bunch of flat-leaf parsley, leaves finely chopped
juice of ½ lemon
2 sheets of filo (phyllo) pastry
sprinkling of caraway seeds (optional)
sea salt and freshly ground black pepper

Preheat the air fryer to 200°C (400°F), removing the crisper plate.

Mix the mushrooms with the garlic and 2 tablespoons of the olive oil, and season well with salt and pepper. Tip into the air fryer and air-fry for 7 minutes, stirring halfway through. Add the spinach and chestnuts, stir well and return to the air fryer for another 4 minutes, until the spinach has defrosted completely.

To make the béchamel, heat a small saucepan over a medium heat, add 2 tablespoons of the olive oil and the flour and whisk together, mixing well to make sure there are no lumps. Carefully pour in the soy milk, whisking all the time. Bring to the boil and continue to whisk until you have a very thick sauce (it should be the consistency of shop-bought custard).

Remove from the heat, then stir in the miso, mustard, parsley and lemon juice, and season well with salt and pepper.

Transfer the mushroom mixture to a cast-iron dish or a cake barrel and stir in the béchamel. Tear the filo (phyllo) pastry into smaller pieces and scrunch on top of the filling – you'll need to tuck the filo pieces in well. Drizzle over the remaining tablespoon of olive oil and sprinkle over the caraway seeds (if using).

Reheat the air fryer to 200°C (400°F) and return to the air fryer for 5 minutes until the filo is golden and crispy. Serve immediately.

Serves 2 generously
–
Prep 15 mins
–
Cook 16 mins

Mains

ALOO GOBI VE

Whole spices make this one-pot dish sing as a stand-alone supper, although you can serve it alongside other curries, with rice or flatbreads or with the grilled cabbages on page 76. If you can get hold of finely chopped canned tomatoes, then do, as they break down more easily.

You will need at least a 5-litre (4½-quart) air fryer to accommodate all the ingredients, as it's important not to let any liquid splash the heating element.

1 small cauliflower, leaves removed, cut into 2cm (¾in) chunks
500g (1lb 2oz) potatoes, cut into 2cm (¾in) chunks (unpeeled)
4 tbsp vegetable oil
2 tsp nigella seeds
1 tsp ground turmeric
1 tsp hot chilli powder
1 tbsp cumin seeds
2 tsp coriander seeds
1 tsp garam masala
150ml (5fl oz/⅔ cup) water
2 × 400g (14oz) cans chopped tomatoes
2 green chillies, deseeded and finely chopped
4 garlic cloves, crushed
thumb-sized piece of fresh root ginger, peeled and finely grated
small bunch of coriander (cilantro), leaves finely chopped
juice of 1 lime
sea salt and freshly ground black pepper

Heat the air fryer to 170°C (340°F), removing the crisper plate.

Mix the cauliflower and potatoes with the oil and all the spices. Tip everything onto the base of the air-fryer basket and pour in the water. Air-fry for 40 minutes, stirring 2 or 3 times during cooking.

Add the tomatoes, chillies, garlic and ginger and stir well. Air-fry for another 25 minutes.

Transfer everything from the air fryer to a serving dish and sprinkle over the chopped coriander (cilantro) and lime juice.

Serve with mango chutney, rice or flatbreads and some coconut yogurt, if you like.

Serves 4
–
Prep 20 mins
–
Cook 65 mins

STUFFED SQUASH VO

This is such an easy recipe and all you need to do is twiddle your thumbs while waiting for the squash to cook. I love cooking squash in an air fryer – it does the job so efficiently. If you want to get ahead, you can fill the squash and leave it to cool. Then just before you want to eat, add the cheese and pop them into the air fryer.

1 butternut or onion squash,
    or Delica pumpkin (750–800g/
    1lb 10oz–1lb 12oz), halved and
    deseeded
1½ tbsp olive oil
140g (5oz) marinated artichokes,
    drained and roughly chopped
100g (3½oz) sun-blush tomatoes,
    roughly chopped
1 × 150g (5½oz) ball of mozzarella
    (or vegan alternative), drained
25g (1oz) pumpkin seeds
sea salt and freshly ground
    black pepper

Preheat the air fryer to 180°C (350°F).

Drizzle the squash halves with 1 tablespoon of the oil and season well with salt and pepper. Place in the air fryer and cook for 50 minutes until the flesh is tender and golden.

Carefully remove the squash from the air fryer and scoop the flesh out into a bowl. Make sure you don't tear the skin of the squash, as you'll be filling it back up!

Mix the artichokes and tomatoes with the cooked squash flesh and season well with salt and pepper. Scoop the mixture back into the empty shells and tear the mozzarella over the top. Return to the air fryer and cook again at 180°C (350°F) for 10 minutes, until the cheese has melted and turned golden.

Meanwhile, toast the pumpkin seeds in a frying pan with the remaining ½ tablespoon of oil until they start to pop and crackle, then season well with salt.

Sprinkle the stuffed squash liberally with the toasted pumpkin seeds and serve immediately.

Serves 2
–
Prep 15 mins
–
Cook 60 mins

SIDES

You'll find the usual suspects here with Piri Piri Fries on page 84, which go nicely with the Black Bean Burgers in the Mains chapter on page 58, and Smashed Baby Potatoes on page 82. For something a little more intriguing, try the Grilled Cabbage with Lime Butter on page 76 or the Braised Fennel on page 88.

BRAISED ROSEMARY POTATOES VE

Potatoes and air fryers are best friends – they just work so well together. These potatoes are crispy and juicy all at once, a mash-up between roast potatoes and pommes boulangère.

300ml (10½fl oz/1¼ cups) hot
  vegetable stock
1 tsp English mustard
2 tsp garlic oil
1kg (2lb 4oz) small potatoes, such
  as Ratte, Anya or Fingerling, cut
  into 5cm (2in) lengths if large
2 large sprigs of rosemary
sea salt

Preheat the air fryer to 180°C (350°F), removing the crisper plate.

Whisk the stock, mustard and garlic oil together and season with salt.

Tip the potatoes onto the base of the air-fryer basket, then pour over the hot liquid. (If you're using an oven-style air fryer or one with a perforated basket, tip everything into a baking tin or cake barrel that fits your air fryer.) Tuck in the rosemary sprigs and air-fry for 45 minutes.

Serve immediately.

Serves 4
–
Prep 5 mins
–
Cook 45 mins

ROASTED SHALLOTS WITH BAY, THYME & ROSEMARY VE

Great on toast for lunch or as a side to a stew with mashed potato, and equally good with veggie sausages or as part of a larger spread of dishes. You can also purée this – just remember to remove the herbs first.

500g (1lb 2oz) banana shallots, peeled and halved lengthways
1 tsp salt
3 tbsp pomegranate molasses
1 tbsp red wine vinegar
1 tbsp olive oil
3 sprigs of thyme
2 sprigs of rosemary
2 bay leaves

Preheat the air fryer to 170°C (340°F).

Mix the shallot halves with the salt, molasses, vinegar and olive oil. Tip into a baking tin (pan) that fits inside your air fryer and tuck in the herbs. Air-fry for 25 minutes until the shallots are soft and caramelized.

Leave to cool a little before serving on top of some toast. Alternatively, remove the herbs and blend the shallots and cooking juices until smooth, then spread on toast!

Serves 4
–
Prep 10 mins
–
Cook 25 mins

GRILLED CABBAGE WITH LIME BUTTER VO

Pointed cabbages work best here as they are sweet and the leaves are tender. This is a riff on a recipe traditionally made on a barbecue, but it works brilliantly in an air fryer. Make sure you don't skip the soaking process, as this traps water in between the leaves and helps the cabbage to cook. Great as a starter or as a side to the Aloo Gobi on page 66. If you have a small air fryer, you'll need to cook these in two batches, as they need to cook in a single layer.

2 small pointed cabbages, washed and outer leaves removed

For the lime butter
100g (3½oz) unsalted butter (or use vegan alternative)
grated zest and juice of 1 lime
1 green or red chilli, deseeded and finely chopped
small bunch of flat-leaf parsley, leaves finely chopped
sea salt and freshly ground black pepper

Cut the cabbages lengthways into quarters, keeping the stalks intact. Cover with cold water and leave to soak for 10 minutes.

Preheat the air fryer to 200°C (400°F).

Drain the cabbage quarters, then place in the air fryer in a single layer – you may need to tuck them in closely to fit everything in. Air-fry for 20 minutes, turning them halfway through to make sure all the sides get nicely charred.

While you wait, make the lime butter. Melt the butter, lime zest and juice and chilli, either in a saucepan over a low heat or in 30-second blasts in the microwave. Remove from the heat, stir in the parsley and season well with salt and pepper. Set aside.

Remove the cabbage from the air fryer and douse each piece with the lime butter – be generous! Serve immediately.

Serves 4
–
Prep 10 mins
–
Cook 20 mins

ROASTED CARROTS WITH PECANS VO

A nice little side that works well alongside the Filo Pie on page 65. If you can get hold of rainbow heritage carrots, then do try them, as they look so pretty on the plate.

800g (1lb 12oz) heritage carrots (or use regular ones), peeled and cut into batons 1cm (½in) thick
3–4 garlic cloves, crushed
a few sprigs of thyme, leaves stripped
2 tbsp soft light or dark brown sugar
60g (2¼oz) butter (or use vegan block), cubed
grated zest and juice of 1 orange
50g (1¾oz) pecans, roughly chopped
sea salt and freshly ground black pepper

Preheat the air fryer to 190°C (375°F), removing the crisper plate.

Add all the ingredients, except the pecans, with salt and pepper to taste, to the base of the air-fryer basket and give everything a good mix. (If you're using an oven-style air fryer or one with a perforated basket, tip everything into a baking tin or cake barrel that fits your air fryer.)

Air-fry for 30 minutes and shake the basket halfway through.

Meanwhile, toast the chopped pecans in a dry frying pan over a high heat for 3–4 minutes until fragrant, stirring frequently so they don't burn.

Remove the carrots and all the cooking juices from the air fryer, scatter over the pecans and serve immediately.

Serves 6
–
Prep 5 mins
–
Cook 30 mins

BALSAMIC ONIONS VO

These would work well alongside the bean burgers on page 58. They are also great as a starter or to keep in the fridge as part of your lunchtime selections.

8 onions, about the size of lemons
3 tbsp extra virgin olive oil
2 tbsp balsamic vinegar
2 large sprigs of rosemary, needles
    stripped, plus extra (optional)
    to serve
100ml (3½fl oz/scant ½ cup) water
crumbled goat's cheese, to serve
    (optional)
sea salt and freshly ground
    black pepper

Cut the tops and tails off the onions but keep most of the papery skin on.

Preheat the air fryer to 185°C (365°F), removing the crisper plate.

Place the onions on the base of the air-fryer basket, making sure they are in a single layer, and drizzle over the extra virgin olive oil and balsamic vinegar. Sprinkle over the rosemary needles and season well with salt and pepper. (If you're using an oven-style air fryer or one with a perforated basket, use a baking tin or cake barrel that fits your air fryer.)

Carefully pour in the water and roast for 40 minutes until the onions are soft but still holding their shape.

Remove, making sure to scrape out any juices, and serve warm with some goat's cheese crumbled over the top, if you like, with extra rosemary.

Serves 4
–
Prep 10 mins
–
Cook 40 mins

SMASHED BABY POTATOES WITH GARLIC & THYME
VE

The potatoes get squashed towards the end of cooking to break up the edges, giving you loads of crispy potato nuggets. This contrasts beautifully with the soft, caramelized garlic.

6–7 sprigs of thyme
1kg (2lb 4oz) baby potatoes, washed
100ml (3½fl oz/scant ½ cup) water
4 tbsp extra virgin olive oil
1 whole bulb of garlic, cloves separated and peeled
sea salt

Preheat the air fryer to 190°C (375°F), removing the crisper plate.

Put the thyme sprigs on the base of your air-fryer basket, then add the potatoes, water and oil – you want to keep the thyme from burning, so make sure the potatoes sit snugly on top. (If you're using an oven-style air fryer or one with a perforated basket, use a baking tin or cake barrel that fits your air fryer.) Air-fry for 30 minutes.

Take a potato masher and squash the potatoes until they are bashed about a bit. Tuck in the garlic cloves and air-fry for another 15 minutes until the potatoes are crispy and the garlic is soft.

Remove, sprinkle over a generous amount of salt and serve immediately.

Serves 4
–
Prep 5 mins
–
Cook 45 mins

PIRI PIRI FRIES VE

No air-fryer book would be complete without a recipe for fries. So here you are! Great served alongside the Black Bean Burgers on page 58.

800g (1lb 12oz) baking potatoes, washed and unpeeled, cut into fries 5mm (¼in) thick
2 tbsp sunflower oil
1 tbsp piri piri seasoning
sea salt
mayonnaise (ensure vegan if needed), to serve

Put the potato fries into a heatproof bowl and pour boiling water over them to cover. Leave to soak for 10 minutes, then drain and pat them dry on kitchen paper or a clean tea towel.

In a bowl, mix the fries with the oil, piri piri seasoning and a little salt.

Preheat the air fryer to 190°C (375°F).

Tip in the fries and air-fry for 35 minutes, shaking the basket a few times during cooking.

Serve immediately, while still hot and crispy, with mayo.

Serves 4
–
Prep 15 mins
–
Cook 35 mins

ROASTED FRENCH BEANS VE

This recipe can be made in the height of summer, when green beans are in plentiful supply, or you can use frozen ones during the winter. These would be delicious served alongside the Singapore Noodles on page 40 or the Filo Pie on page 65.

1 tbsp olive or vegetable oil
1 tbsp toasted sesame oil
2 garlic cloves, crushed
2 tbsp soy sauce
500g (1lb 2oz) fresh or frozen French beans, tailed
1 tbsp sesame seeds
sea salt and freshly ground black pepper

Preheat the air fryer to 200°C (400°F), removing the crisper plate.

In a bowl, mix the oils, garlic and soy sauce together, then season with a pinch of salt and some black pepper. Mix with the green beans, then add to the base of the air-fryer basket. (If you're using an oven-style air fryer or one with a perforated basket, tip everything into a baking tin or cake barrel that fits your air fryer.)

Air-fry for 8 minutes, then stir in the sesame seeds and air-fry for another 3 minutes, until the beans have browned a bit and the seeds have toasted.

Best enjoyed warm or at room temperature.

Serves 4
–
Prep 5 mins
–
Cook 11 mins

BRAISED FENNEL VE

A few simple ingredients go into this dish, which is a bit like confit fennel – sweet and soft, with a delicious saffron cooking liquor. The secret is cooking the fennel in a cake barrel for quite a long time to give you a tender side dish – not something you would expect from an air fryer! This keeps well in the fridge for a few days.

2 fennel bulbs, halved, fronds reserved and chopped
200ml (7fl oz/scant 1 cup) vegan white wine
200ml (7fl oz/scant 1 cup) hot vegetable stock
4 tbsp extra virgin olive oil
pinch of saffron strands
2 tbsp caster (superfine) sugar
1 tsp sea salt

Preheat the air fryer to 180°C (350°F).

Arrange the fennel halves snugly in a cake barrel, in a single layer if possible, but don't worry if they overlap a bit.

Heat the wine, stock, oil, saffron, sugar and salt in a small saucepan until it comes to a boil, then pour over the fennel. Try and make sure all the fennel is submerged, but don't worry if some bits stick out.

Pop the cake barrel into the air fryer and bake the fennel for 50 minutes, turning the pieces over halfway through; they will soften as they braise.

Remove and serve the fennel with the reserved chopped fronds sprinkled on top.

Serves 4
–
Prep 5 mins
–
Cook 50 mins

RUNNER BEANS WITH CREAM & ALMONDS VO

This dish can be served as a side or even as a sauce for pasta, or a filling for a baked potato. I feel like runner beans aren't that popular these days, as they require de-stringing, but I remember my mum growing them and I would help her prepare them each summer, so this recipe pays homage to her. If you can't get hold of runner beans, use flat green beans or even French beans.

500g (1lb 2oz) fresh or frozen runner beans, destringed and cut on the diagonal into 1cm (½in) slices if using fresh
150g (5½oz) double (heavy) cream (or vegan alternative)
1 garlic clove, crushed
50g (1¾oz) flaked (slivered) almonds
small bunch of flat-leaf parsley, leaves finely chopped
grated Parmesan or Pecorino (or use vegan alternative), to serve
sea salt and freshly ground black pepper

Preheat the air fryer to 180°C (350°F).

In a bowl, mix the beans with the cream and garlic and season well with salt and pepper.

Tip into a cake barrel or similar receptacle and air-fry for 8 minutes, stirring halfway through.

Meanwhile, dry-fry (no oil required here!) the almonds in a frying pan over a high heat for 2–3 minutes until golden and toasted.

Remove the creamy beans from the air fryer and stir through the parsley. Sprinkle over some freshly grated Parmesan or Pecorino and the toasted almonds, and serve.

Serves 4
–
Prep 8 mins
–
Cook 5 mins

AUBERGINE WITH OREGANO & PINE NUTS VE

A lovely caponata-style side, this will keep in the fridge for a week or so and can be eaten cold as well as at room temperature. You could turn this into a snack by serving it on top of some toasted ciabatta. Or it would also be good alongside the mushroom rolls on page 113 or the Loaded Fries on page 110.

1 onion, finely sliced
4 tbsp olive oil
2 aubergines (eggplants), cut into
 1cm (½in) dice
2 garlic cloves, finely sliced
2 tbsp nonpareil salted capers,
 rinsed to remove the salt
1 × 400g (14oz) can chopped tomatoes
2 tbsp balsamic vinegar
6 sprigs of fresh oregano, leaves
 finely chopped
1 tbsp soft brown sugar
50g (1¾oz) pine nuts
sea salt and freshly ground
 black pepper

Preheat the air fryer to 180°C (350°F).

Put the onion and 2 tablespoons of the olive oil into a cake barrel or similar receptacle and set it inside the air-fryer basket. Air-fry for 8 minutes until soft and slightly browned, stirring a couple of times during cooking.

Add the aubergine (eggplant), garlic and the remaining 2 tablespoons of olive oil to the onion. Season well with salt and pepper and give everything a good stir. Return to the air fryer for 10 minutes.

Lower the temperature of the air fryer to 170°C (340°F). Add the capers, chopped tomatoes, balsamic vinegar, oregano and sugar to the cake barrel and stir well. Return to the air fryer and cook for 30 minutes until everything is dark, sticky and soft, stirring a few times during cooking.

Meanwhile, to toast the pine nuts, heat a dry frying pan over a high heat and toast the nuts for 2–3 minutes until golden. Keep stirring them and don't get distracted or leave them, otherwise they will burn!

Top the aubergine with the toasted pine nuts and serve.

Serves 4
as a side
–
Prep 10 mins
–
Cook 48 mins

SNACKS

These recipes are all perfect for sharing with others, like the baked feta on page 108, but you can enjoy them by yourself if you're ravenous. Sometimes you just need a plate of Loaded Fries (page 110) all to yourself...

GOCHUJANG, CAULIFLOWER & TOFU SKEWERS VE

Sweet and spicy, tender tofu and chewy cauliflower: these won't last long once they've been served up. Instead of making them as a snack to serve four, you could prepare them as a lunch for two people, with a crunchy Asian slaw on the side.

120g (4¼oz) plain (all-purpose) flour
1 tsp onion granules
200ml (7fl oz/scant 1 cup) water
1 small cauliflower, cut into
   bite-sized florets
1 × 369g (13oz) block of firm tofu,
   drained, patted dry and cut into
   2cm (¾in) cubes
sea salt

For the glaze
4 tbsp gochujang paste
2 tbsp golden syrup
1 tbsp rice vinegar
2 tbsp soy sauce
2 garlic cloves, crushed
3cm (1¼in) piece of fresh root ginger,
   peeled and finely grated
2 tbsp water

To serve
3 spring onions (scallions), finely sliced
about 1 tbsp sesame seeds

If necessary, trim 8 wooden skewers to fit your air fryer so they lie flat. Soak the skewers in cold water while you prepare the recipe.

In a large bowl, whisk together the flour, onion granules and water along with a pinch of salt. Tip the cauliflower and tofu in and carefully mix everything together, trying not to break up the tofu.

Remove the skewers from the water, then thread the cauliflower and tofu onto the skewers in any order you like.

Preheat the air fryer to 190°C (375°F) and cook 4 skewers at a time, for 15 minutes, turning halfway through. If you have a 2-drawer air fryer you can use both drawers to cook all 8 skewers at once.

Meanwhile, in a bowl, whisk all the glaze ingredients together.

Once the skewers have all cooked, brush them liberally with the glaze and return to the air fryer for 3 minutes. Again, this is best done in batches.

Serve immediately with spring onions (scallions) and sesame seeds scattered over the top.

Serves 4
–
Prep 15 mins
–
Cook 36 mins

Snacks

SWEETCORN & EDAMAME FRITTERS

Frozen sweetcorn and edamame beans work best here, otherwise the mixture becomes too wet. You can use canned or ready-to-eat, but just ensure they are very well drained.

150g (5½oz) plain (all-purpose) flour
1 garlic clove, crushed
85ml (3fl oz/⅓ cup) milk
2 medium eggs, beaten
3 spring onions (scallions),
    finely chopped
small bunch of dill, finely chopped,
    plus extra to serve
handful of mint leaves, finely chopped,
    plus extra to serve
200g (7oz) frozen sweetcorn
200g (7oz) frozen edamame beans
olive oil, for drizzling
sea salt and freshly ground
    black pepper

To serve
1 avocado, sliced
drizzle of extra virgin olive oil

Preheat the air fryer to 200°C (400°F).

In a bowl, whisk together the flour, garlic, milk and eggs until smooth, then stir in the spring onions (scallions), dill, mint, sweetcorn and edamame beans until well combined. Season with some salt and pepper.

Line the air-fryer basket with baking parchment, then spoon large blobs of batter onto it, spreading them out slightly but keeping them spaced apart. You should be able to cook 4 fritters at a time (or more if you have a 2-drawer air fryer). Drizzle over a little olive oil and air-fry for 15 minutes, turning them over halfway through.

Repeat with any remaining batter.

Serve with avocado slices, more dill and mint and a drizzle of extra virgin olive oil.

Serves 4
–
Prep 5 mins
–
Cook 30 mins

SAMOSAS VE

My dad loves samosas, and when I was a child I remember him eating them standing up in the kitchen – the pastry falling all over the place as he crunched them up with wild abandon! He first showed me how to eat them with loads of lemon squeezed over the top, and so this recipe is for him. It's a good idea to use a cake barrel for the first part of this recipe to save cleaning the air fryer halfway through.

5 tbsp olive oil
1 onion, finely chopped
2 green chillies, deseeded and finely chopped
5cm (2in) piece of fresh root ginger, peeled and grated
2 garlic cloves, crushed
1 medium potato, peeled and finely chopped into 3mm (⅛in) cubes
1 tbsp mild curry powder
good pinch each of sea salt and freshly ground black pepper
1 tbsp water
100g (3½oz) frozen peas, defrosted
small bunch of coriander (cilantro), leaves finely chopped
3 large sheets filo (phyllo) pastry (about 45 × 30cm/18 × 12in)
1 tbsp nigella seeds
lemon wedges, to serve

Preheat the air fryer to 190°C (375°F).

Pour 1 tablespoon of the oil into a cake barrel, then add the onion, chilli, ginger and garlic. Put the cake barrel in the air fryer and cook for 8 minutes, stirring halfway through.

Add the potato, curry powder, salt, pepper and water, stir and return to the air fryer for another 10 minutes. Remove the cake barrel and stir in the peas and coriander (cilantro). Set aside to cool briefly.

Prepare the pastry: stack the filo (phyllo) sheets on top of each other, then cut them in half lengthways and separate them – you'll end up with 6 strips about 12 × 45cm (4¾ × 18in). It doesn't matter if they are a bit shorter but you do need them to be at least 12cm (4¾in) wide to hold all the filling.

Lay one strip of filo in portrait on a work surface. Spoon a heaped tablespoon of the filling onto the bottom fifth of the pastry. Fold the bottom right-hand corner of the pastry over the filling to the left-hand side, making a triangle shape, then fold the pastry up, enclosing the filling. Repeat by folding the pastry from left to right this time and continue folding in this way until you reach the end of the strip. Brush the end of the pastry with olive oil before folding to seal, then brush the whole samosa with more oil. Set aside and repeat this process with the remaining filling and pastry.

Sprinkle with the nigella seeds, then bake in the air fryer at 190°C (375°F) for 8 minutes. Serve with lemon wedges, for squeezing over.

Makes 6
–
Prep 15 mins
–
Cook 26 mins

Snacks

101

SEEDED CRACKERS WITH BEETROOT & DILL DIP VE

Don't buy crackers – make them instead! These are insanely good, and a bit like the shop-bought ones you can find in some delis. They keep for ages in an airtight container and are vegan and gluten-free to boot... If you have a small air fryer, you'll need to bake these in two batches. If you have a 2-drawer air fryer you might find it easier to split the dough in half and utilise both drawers at the same time. Make sure you cook these on the crisper plate so the air circulates evenly around the cracker dough.

For the crackers
100g (3½oz) mixed seeds
2 tbsp ground flaxseed
4 tbsp gram flour
1 tsp sea salt
1 tbsp extra virgin olive oil
3 tbsp water

For the beetroot and dill dip
125g (4½oz) cooked beetroot (beet)
small bunch of dill
juice of 1 lemon
1 garlic clove, crushed
1 × 215g (7½oz) can chickpeas, drained
1 tbsp extra virgin olive oil
sea salt and freshly ground
    black pepper

Mix all the cracker ingredients in a bowl to make a dough. Leave to sit for 10 minutes so the flaxseed can absorb all the water.

Roll the dough between 2 pieces of baking parchment into a square or circle about 3mm (⅛in) thick. Peel off the top layer of parchment and cut away the exposed edges of the bottom piece (this means the air can circulate around the dough to give an even bake).

Preheat the air fryer to 170°C (340°F).

Carefully place the dough in the air fryer, making sure it stays as flat as possible, but a few creases or wrinkles won't matter. Bake for 25 minutes until crisp and golden brown. Remove from the air fryer, leave to cool, then break into shards.

To make the dip, blitz all the ingredients in a food processor or using a stick blender until smooth, adding salt and pepper to taste, then transfer to a serving bowl and serve alongside the cracker shards.

Serves 4
–
Prep 15 mins
–
Cook 25 mins

COURGETTE FALAFEL WITH TAHINI SAUCE VO

These work as part of a larger collection of snacks, or are equally good as a starter. They are softer than regular falafel, but so easy to make, and feel quite virtuous to eat!

1 large (300g/10½oz) courgette
    (zucchini), coarsely grated
1 × 400g (14oz) can cannellini
    beans, drained
75g (2½oz) plain (all-purpose) flour
small bunch each of dill, mint and
    parsley, leaves finely chopped
juice of ½ lemon
a little olive oil, for brushing
sea salt and freshly ground
    black pepper

To serve
200g (7oz/scant 1 cup) Greek yogurt
    (or vegan alternative)
3 tbsp tahini
1 garlic clove, crushed
juice of 1 lemon

Mix the grated courgette (zucchini) with a generous sprinkling of salt, then place in a sieve (strainer) set over a bowl to drain. Leave for 10 minutes, then squeeze out as much excess water as you can.

Meanwhile, in a bowl, mash the cannellini beans until you have a lumpy mash, then stir in the flour, herbs and lemon juice. Season with black pepper and a pinch more salt, then stir in the squeezed courgettes.

Divide the mixture into about 12 and shape into small golf-ball-sized balls, then brush them all with oil.

Preheat the air fryer to 190°C (375°F).

Brush the crisper plate with a little oil and air-fry the falafel for 15 minutes, turning halfway through.

To make the tahini dip, mix the yogurt with the tahini, garlic, lemon juice and a pinch of salt, to give a thick sauce. Add a little water if it's too dry.

Remove the falafel from the air fryer and serve with the dip.

Serves 4
–
Prep 20 mins
–
Cook 15 mins

SPINACH & FETA BOREK

I first tasted these in one of my local cafés. They were made into long cigar shapes, and my step-daughter and I couldn't get enough of them! I created this recipe for her, but here I've made them into parcels so you can fit more in the air fryer. They can be made ahead and enjoyed at room temperature.

5 sheets of filo (phyllo) pastry
160g (5½oz) baby leaf spinach
1 medium egg
50g (1¾oz) mascarpone
200g (7oz) feta, crumbled
50g (1¾oz) butter, melted
1 tbsp sesame seeds
sea salt and freshly ground
    black pepper

Cut the filo (phyllo) sheets in half, giving you 10 squares roughly 20cm (8in). It doesn't matter if yours are slightly larger. Cover with a damp tea towel to prevent them from drying out.

Put the spinach into a large heatproof bowl and cover with boiling water. Leave for 5 minutes to wilt, then drain, squeeze out any excess liquid and roughly chop.

In a separate bowl, whisk the egg with the mascarpone and feta. Season with a little salt and lots of black pepper, then mix in the chopped spinach.

Take 2 sheets of filo pastry (keep the rest under the damp tea towel) and brush one with melted butter. Stack the other on top and brush this with more melted butter.

Dollop 2 tablespoons of the spinach and feta mixture into the centre of the bottom third of the filo square, then fold the pastry up and over the mixture. Tuck both sides in and roll the pastry up, enclosing the filling to make a large spring-roll shape. Brush with more melted butter and sprinkle over some sesame seeds.

Repeat this process with the remaining pastry and filling to make 5 parcels in total.

Preheat the air fryer to 180°C (350°F).

Lay a sheet of perforated baking parchment on the crisper plate in the air fryer, then bake the borek parcels, spaced apart and seam side down, for 20 minutes. Leave for about 10 minutes to cool before tucking in.

Serves 5
–
Prep 25 mins
–
Cook 20 mins

Snacks

BAKED FETA WITH SPICED TOMATO SAUCE

VO

A lovely little saganaki dish, perfect for putting in the middle of the table to share. Your choice of chilli flakes will change the dish – try smoky chipotle for a deep flavour, or Aleppo pepper for a fruity, warm, mild spice. You'll need a deep baking tin (pan) which fits inside your air fryer – I made this in an 18 × 22 × 5cm (7 × 8¾ x 2in) tin.

2 ready-to-bake small ciabattas
1 red onion, finely sliced
2 garlic cloves, crushed
3 tbsp extra virgin olive oil, plus an
   extra drizzle
1 tsp dried oregano
½ tsp chilli (red pepper) flakes of
   choice (see recipe introduction)
2 × 400g (14oz) cans cherry tomatoes
1 × 200g (7oz) block of feta (or vegan
   alternative), drained
a little runny honey (or maple syrup
   if making it vegan)
sea salt and freshly ground
   black pepper

Preheat the air fryer to 180°C (350°F). Bake the ciabattas in the air fryer for 8 minutes. Remove and leave to cool for a few minutes before cutting into chunks or slices.

Increase the temperature of the air fryer to 190°C (375°F).

Put the onion in a baking tin (pan) along with the garlic, oil, oregano, chilli (red pepper) flakes and some salt and pepper, and air-fry for 8 minutes, stirring halfway through. Add the tomatoes, give it all a good stir and air-fry for another 5 minutes.

Take the whole block of feta and tuck it into the middle of the sauce. Drizzle with a little olive oil and air-fry for another 9 minutes.

Remove and drizzle over a little runny honey, then serve in the tin with the ciabatta alongside.

Serves 4–6
–
Prep 10 mins
–
Cook 31 mins

LOADED FRIES

This isn't pretty but it's so delicious to eat! I recommend devouring it while wearing your pyjamas (or all by yourself standing at the kitchen counter...).

500g (1lb 2oz) store-bought frozen
   sweet potato fries
1 small red onion, finely chopped
a few pickled jalapeños, chopped
1 tbsp olive oil
100g (3½oz) Gruyère, grated
50g (1¾oz) Emmental, grated
1 avocado, halved, pitted and flesh
   finely chopped
small bunch of coriander (cilantro),
   leaves finely chopped
juice of 1 lime
chilli ketchup, to serve
sea salt and freshly ground
   black pepper

Preheat the air fryer to 190°C (375°F).

Tip the fries into the air fryer and arrange in a single layer so they all cook evenly. Air-fry for 10 minutes.

Meanwhile, mix together the onion, jalapeños, olive oil and some salt and pepper to taste.

Top the cooked fries with the grated cheeses and onion mixture in a few alternating layers. Return to the air fryer for another 5 minutes until the cheese is melted and starting to colour.

Tumble everything onto a serving dish, scatter over the chopped avocado and coriander (cilantro) and drizzle over the lime juice. Dig in, with chilli ketchup on the side.

Serves 2
–
Prep 5 mins
–
Cook 15 mins

MUSHROOM & LENTIL ROLLS VE

These are packed with plants and will satisfy your craving for a 'meaty' sausage roll. If you are lucky enough to have a 2-drawer air fryer, you can cook these in a single batch, taking the overall cooking time down to under half an hour.

2 banana shallots, roughly chopped
300g (10½oz) mixed mushrooms
3 sprigs of thyme, leaves picked
1 garlic clove, crushed
1 tbsp olive oil
2 tbsp crunchy peanut butter
1 tbsp brown rice miso
1 tbsp wholegrain mustard
125g (4½oz) cooked Beluga lentils
50g (1¾oz) cooked chestnuts, crumbled
½ bunch of flat-leaf parsley, leaves
    finely chopped
1 × 320g (11oz) sheet of ready-rolled
    vegan puff pastry
1–2 tbsp plant-based milk, for brushing
smoked chilli ketchup, to serve
sea salt and freshly ground
    black pepper

Put the shallots, mushrooms, thyme and garlic into a food processor and blitz until finely chopped, but don't run the processor for too long or they will turn to mush!

Preheat the air fryer to 190°C (375°F), removing the crisper plate.

Put the finely chopped mushroom mixture on the base of the air-fryer basket and drizzle over the olive oil. (If you're using an oven-style air fryer or one with a perforated basket, tip everything into a baking tin or cake barrel that fits your air fryer.) Season with salt and pepper, then air-fry for 13 minutes, until golden and most of the liquid has evaporated, stirring halfway through.

While the mushrooms are cooking, in a bowl, mix together the peanut butter, miso and mustard, then stir together with the lentils, chestnuts and parsley, making sure everything is well mixed. Once the mushrooms have finished cooking, add them to the lentil mixture, stir well and set aside to cool for a few minutes.

Unroll the sheet of puff pastry and cut in half widthways, giving you 2 squares.

Spoon half the mixture down one side of a square in a long sausage, then roll it up into a sausage-roll shape. Brush a little milk on the edge to seal, then turn over and brush the tops with more milk. Cut into 4 sausage rolls and set aside. Repeat this process with the remaining pastry and mushroom mixture.

Reheat the air fryer back to 190°C (375°F), this time with the crisper plate inside. Place 4 rolls on the plate, spaced apart, and air-fry for 15 minutes. Repeat with the remaining 4 rolls.

Remove and leave to cool for a few minutes before serving, with smoked chilli ketchup on the side.

> **Serves 4**
> –
> **Prep 20 mins**
> –
> **Cook 43 mins, for 2 batches**

RED PEPPER DIP WITH FLATBREADS VO

This is inspired by both the North African cooked tomato salad matbucha, and the Spanish sauce romesco: sweet, tangy and spicy all at once, with plenty of punchy flavours. Here you make the flatbreads in a frying pan and use them to scoop up the tangy (bell) pepper salad. Roasting red peppers in an air fryer works so well, so I hope you give this a try.

1 red (bell) pepper, halved
    and deseeded
3 medium tomatoes, halved
25g (1oz) flaked (slivered) almonds
1 tbsp extra virgin olive oil
½ tbsp gochujang or chilli paste
1 tsp hot smoked paprika
1 tbsp sherry vinegar
1 garlic clove, crushed
sea salt and freshly ground
    black pepper

For the flatbreads
150g (5½oz) self-raising flour,
    plus extra for dusting
150g (5½oz) Greek yogurt
    (or vegan alternative)
pinch of salt

Preheat the air fryer to 200°C (400°F), removing the crisper plate.

Season the (bell) peppers and tomato halves with salt, then place them on the base of the air-fryer basket, cut side down. (If you're using an oven-style air fryer or one with a perforated basket, place in a baking tin or cake barrel that fits your air fryer.) Roast for 15 minutes until the skins have blackened in places and the vegetables have softened.

Transfer the peppers and tomatoes to a bowl, discarding the cooking juices, and cover with a plate or cling film (plastic wrap). Leave for 10 minutes to steam, which will make the skins easier to remove.

Toast the almonds in a dry frying pan over a medium heat for 3–4 minutes until golden brown; stir frequently and don't take your eyes off them, as they can burn easily! Set aside.

Add the olive oil, gochujang, paprika, vinegar and garlic to another mixing bowl and season well with salt and pepper.

Once the peppers and tomatoes are cool enough to handle, peel off the skins and finely chop the flesh. Add the flesh to the mixing bowl and stir well before transferring to a serving dish and sprinkling over the toasted almonds.

To make the flatbreads, stir together the flour, yogurt and salt in a bowl, until you have a ball of dough. Bring the last bits together with your hands and knead for 5 minutes until smooth. Leave to rest for 15 minutes to allow the dough to relax (so you can roll them out more easily). Divide into 4–6 balls, then roll each out on a floured surface to about 5mm (¼in) thick. Heat a frying pan (no need for any oil here!) over a high heat, then fry the flatbreads, a couple at a time, for 2–3 minutes on each side. They should puff up a little and have blackened spots on each side.

Serve the warm flatbreads with the pepper dip.

Serves 4–6
–
Prep 20 mins
–
Cook 15 mins

SWEET THINGS

This chapter is packed with plants and makes good use of your spice rack too. The flapjacks on page 126 have parsnips and ginger in them, and the brownies on page 123 contain cardamom and beetroot. For a really indulgent treat, try the Spiced Bread & Butter Pudding on Page 134.

RASPBERRY COBBLER VO

A delightful little pudding that the kids will enjoy, and using frozen berries means you can make this year-round. The combination of flavours is just like a raspberry coconut slice. I make this in a 20cm (8in) cake barrel, which is 9cm (3½in) deep, so use a similar-sized dish.

400g (14oz) frozen raspberries
1 tbsp cornflour (cornstarch)
30g (1oz) caster (superfine) sugar
a few drops of vanilla extract
plain yogurt, double (heavy) cream
   or custard (or vegan alternative),
   to serve

For the cobbler topping
100g (3½oz) self-raising flour
30g (1oz) desiccated (dried
   shredded) coconut
30g (1oz) caster (superfine) sugar
50g (1¾oz) cold butter (or vegan
   block), cut into small cubes
65ml (2¼fl oz/generous ¼ cup) whole
   milk (or vegan alternative)
a few drops of almond extract

Preheat your air fryer to 190°C (375°F).

In a bowl, mix together the frozen raspberries with the cornflour (cornstarch), sugar and vanilla extract. Break up any raspberries that are stuck together to ensure they are all coated in sugar and cornflour. Pour into a cake barrel that fits inside your air fryer.

For the topping, mix together the flour, coconut and sugar. Rub the butter (or vegan block) in with your fingertips until it looks like breadcrumbs – don't worry if you still have some lumps of butter. Pour in the milk and almond extract and mix together with a knife, fork or spoon until it just comes together. Dollop spoonfuls of the mixture in blobs on top of the raspberries (the topping won't totally cover the raspberries, which is fine) and air-fry for 18 minutes until the topping has puffed up and turned a golden brown, and the berries are bubbling and syrupy.

Serve immediately with yogurt, cream or ice cream.

Serves 4
–
Prep 15 mins
–
Cook 18 mins

ORANGE SHORTBREAD

Semolina makes these shortbread biscuits (cookies) extra crunchy – perfect for dunking in a cup of tea. The dough is freezable and you can slice off rounds and bake them from frozen (a bit like cookie dough). A nifty recipe for unannounced visitors you'd like to impress. You'll need a perforated parchment liner.

150g (5½oz) soft unsalted butter
70g (2½oz) caster (superfine) sugar
grated zest of 1 orange
150g (5½oz) plain (all-purpose) flour, plus extra for dusting
70g (2½oz) fine semolina

In a bowl, cream together the butter, sugar and orange zest until light and fluffy. Stir in the flour and semolina and bring together into a ball of dough. I like to use my hands towards the end, as it's easier than using a wooden spoon.

Tip the dough out onto a work surface dusted lightly with flour and shape into a long sausage roughly 5cm (2in) in diameter.

Wrap the sausage tightly in baking parchment and chill in the fridge for 30 minutes. (You can freeze the dough at this stage and cut discs to bake as and when you want them.)

Remove the dough from the fridge and preheat the air fryer to 165°C (330°F).

Cut discs 5mm (¼in) thick and place them, spaced apart, on a perforated parchment liner on the crisper plate to allow the air to circulate. You will likely have to cook them in batches – I can fit 12–15 at a time in my air fryer – although if you have a 2-drawer air fryer you may be able to cook them all at once. Bake for 14 minutes, until just golden on top.

Carefully remove the shortbread biscuits from the air fryer by sliding them, still on the perforated liner, onto a wire rack (so you don't break any of them). Leave to cool and set before serving with a pot of tea.

Makes about 32
–
Prep 20 mins
–
Chill 30 mins
–
Cook 14 mins

Sweet Things

BEETROOT & CARDAMOM BROWNIES

Beetroot (beet) and cocoa are a match made in heaven, and these brownies are spiced with cardamom, making them feel fancy. They are cakey rather than fudgey, and quite rich, so you only need a small slice to satisfy your chocolate craving. As they are made with dark chocolate, which has more fibre in it, and a little flaxseed, which contains omega 3, you can feel virtuous while you are snacking! They are very good served with a glass of cold milk. You bake these in a 20cm (8in) sandwich tin on top of the crisper plate to ensure the air circulates for an even bake.

seeds of 4 green cardamom pods
    or ¼ tsp ground green cardamom
125g (4½oz) unsalted butter, cubed
100g (3½oz) 70% dark chocolate,
    broken into pieces
2 eggs
100g (3½oz) caster (superfine) sugar
100g (3½oz) cooked beetroot
    (beet), grated
80g (2¾oz) plain (all-purpose) flour
20g (¾oz) unsweetened cocoa powder
20g (¾oz) ground flaxseed

If using whole cardamom pods, crush the pods in a pestle and mortar and remove the green casing. Crush the seeds as finely as you can.

Put the butter, chocolate and crushed/ground cardamom in a heatproof bowl set over a pan of simmering water, and allow the butter and chocolate to melt. You can also do this in the microwave in 30-second blasts.

In a separate bowl, beat together the eggs and sugar until combined. Pour over the melted chocolate mixture, tip in the grated beetroot (beet) and beat again.

Preheat the air fryer to 170°C (340°F) and line a 20cm (8in) baking tin (pan) with baking parchment.

Sift together the flour and cocoa and fold through the mixture, then stir in the flaxseed. Pour into the prepared tin, levelling out the top with the back of a spoon. Transfer to the air fryer and air-fry for 25 minutes until puffed up and set.

Leave to cool in the tin, then cut into 8 slices and enjoy.

Makes 8
–
Prep 10 mins
–
Cook 25 mins

Sweet Things

ROASTED PEAR CHARLOTTE

This turns out like a pear pie, with golden crusty bread encasing soft, sweet pears. It can be cooled and cut into slices, or eaten warm with the juices oozing out.

7 Medjool dates, pitted and
finely chopped
80ml (2¾fl oz/⅓ cup) boiling water
80g (2¾oz) butter, cut into cubes
4 ripe pears, peeled, cored and
quartered
grated zest and juice of 1 lemon
3 tbsp demerara (turbinado) sugar
8 slices of soft white bread,
crusts removed
crème fraîche, to serve

Preheat the air fryer to 170°C (340°F).

Add the dates to a heatproof bowl, pour over the boiling water and leave to soak for 5 minutes.

Put 60g (2¼oz) of the cubed butter into a cake barrel with the pears, lemon zest and juice and the dates and their soaking water. Air-fry for 15 minutes, until the pears are soft, stirring 2 or 3 times during cooking.

Meanwhile, melt the remaining butter in the microwave for 10 seconds. Brush the base and sides of a 20cm (8in) baking tin (pan) with half the melted butter and sprinkle over half the sugar.

Roll out the bread slices until they are slightly flattened, then layer 7 of them in the dish, slightly overlapping the slices and making sure they come up the sides and over the edges of the tin, so you have bread to fold over the top.

Once the pears have had their time, spoon them into the bread case along with all the juices. Fold the overhanging bread over the top and add the remaining slice of bread to enclose the filling.

Brush the top with the remaining butter, sprinkle over the remaining sugar and cook in the air fryer for 15 minutes.

Remove and leave to cool slightly before serving in wedges, with some crème fraîche.

Serves 4
–
Prep 25 mins
–
Cook 30 mins

PARSNIP FLAPJACKS VE

Chewy, spiced and filling, these flapjacks are a great lunchbox filler as well as being useful for restoring your fuel tank after a workout. This recipe makes about 8 bars, depending on how you cut them, and they keep for a few days in a tightly shut container. Parsnips work nicely in sweet dishes, as they are naturally sweet themselves, plus they contribute to the chewy texture.

100g (3½oz) parsnip (about 1 medium), peeled and finely grated
125g (4½oz) porridge oats
½ tsp ground ginger
1 tsp ground cinnamon
1 tbsp ground flaxseed
pinch of salt
2 tbsp sunflower oil
120g (4¼oz) golden syrup
2 tsp vanilla extract
1 tbsp crunchy hazelnut or almond butter

For the topping
50g (1¾oz) dark chocolate, broken into pieces
1 tbsp crunchy hazelnut or almond butter

Preheat the air fryer to 180°C (350°F). Line an 18 × 22cm (7 × 8¾in) baking tin (pan) with baking parchment.

In a bowl, mix the grated parsnip, oats, ginger, cinnamon, flaxseed and salt together. In a separate bowl, mix the oil, syrup, vanilla and nut butter until amalgamated and gloopy. Combine the dry and wet ingredients until well combined.

Pour the mixture into the lined tin and flatten out, pressing down to make an even layer.

Air-fry for 20 minutes until golden on top and set.

To make the topping, put the chocolate and nut butter in a heatproof bowl and set it over a pan of barely simmering water until just melted, then set aside. You can also do this in a microwave in 30-second bursts.

Carefully remove the tin from the air fryer, keeping the flapjacks in the tin, then cut into bars while still warm. Drizzle over the nutty chocolate topping and leave to cool, then devour!

Makes 8
–
Prep 10 mins
–
Cook 20 mins

APPLE STREUSEL CAKE

My step-mum, Jennifer, is a fantastic cook and a great baker. She has a small orchard at the top of her garden and I thought of her while writing this recipe; I hope it's as good as her cakes are. Apple cake is my favourite – I love the burst of fruity chunks you get with each mouthful, and the apple helps to prevent the cake from drying out. You will need a cake tin (pan) that fits inside your air fryer with some space around the edges to ensure the air circulates.

150g (5½oz) plain (all-purpose) flour
1 tsp baking powder
½ tsp ground cinnamon
½ tsp ground ginger
2 eating apples, peeled, cored and
    finely chopped
60g (2¼oz) unsalted butter, softened,
    plus extra for greasing
100g (3½oz) caster (superfine) sugar
1 large egg, beaten
½ tsp vanilla extract
100ml (3½fl oz/scant ½ cup) milk
chilled double (heavy) cream, to serve

For the topping
40g (1½oz) cold unsalted butter, cubed
50g (1¾oz) demerara (turbinado) sugar
60g (2¼oz) plain (all-purpose) flour
1 tsp ground cinnamon
50g (1¾oz) mixed nuts,
    roughly chopped
1 heaped tbsp jumbo oats

Grease a 20cm (8in) cake tin (pan) and line it with baking parchment.

Sift together the flour, baking powder and ground spices, then stir in the chopped apples and set aside.

In a separate bowl, beat together the butter and sugar until creamy and light, then add the egg, bit by bit, until combined. Whisk in the vanilla extract and milk, then fold in the flour and apple mixture until combined. Make sure there are no hidden lumps of flour, then pour the batter into the lined tin, smoothing out the top to make it as level as possible.

Now make the streusel topping. Using your fingertips, rub the butter with the sugar, flour and cinnamon until you have a crumble-like mixture, then stir in the nuts and oats.

Preheat the air fryer to 160°C (325°F).

Spoon the streusel over the top of the batter, then carefully place the tin inside the air fryer (on top of the crisper plate) and bake for 40 minutes.

Serve in wedges with some very cold cream.

Serves 8
–
Prep 25 mins
–
Cook 40 mins

BAKED APPLES WITH CHERRIES

VO

This is a lovely autumnal pudding; the cherries will remind you of warmer summer days and, if you use the Amaretto, you can steal a sip while you're preparing the pudding. Make sure you score each apple or they will burst all over your air fryer!

3 tbsp cherry compôte
2 shop-bought madeleines, crumbled
50g (1¾oz) soft light brown sugar
35g (1¼oz) soft butter (or vegan block)
6 small, red apples, cored and scored around the middle
200g (7oz) frozen cherries
a few drops of almond extract
2 tbsp Amaretto (optional)
vanilla ice cream or double (heavy) cream (or vegan alternatives), to serve

Mix together the cherry compote with the madeleine crumbs, sugar and butter (or vegan block). Stuff each cored apple with this mixture – it will spill out over the top a little.

Mix the frozen cherries with the almond extract and Amaretto (if using).

Pour the frozen cherries into the base of the cold air-fryer basket, then sit the apples, cores pointing up, on top.

Close the drawer and set the air fryer to 180°C (350°F). Bake for 25 minutes until the apples are soft but still holding their shape and the cherries have made a syrupy sauce.

Remove and set aside to cool briefly, as they can be too hot to eat immediately. Serve with ice cream or cream on the side.

Serves 6
–
Prep 15 mins
–
Cook 25 mins

RHUBARB CRUMBLE VE

Best made with the forced rhubarb that comes along in January; it's delicately pink and sweeter than the summer stuff, which feels decadent in the cold winter months. Somehow the colour and tang brighten up those wintry days. Having said that, I would still make this in the summer!

400g (14oz) forced rhubarb, cut into
   even lengths, about 2.5cm (1in)
1 tbsp cornflour (cornstarch)
125g (4½oz) soft light brown sugar
4 cardamom pods, bashed
1 wide, pared strip of lemon zest
juice of 2 oranges (grate and reserve
   the zest for the crumble)
1 tsp vanilla bean paste
vegan vanilla or chocolate ice cream,
   to serve

For the crumble
80g (2¾oz) jumbo oats
80g (2¾oz) soft light brown sugar
80g (2¾oz) plain (all-purpose) flour
40g (1½oz) fine polenta
grated zest of 2 oranges
80g (2¾oz) cold vegan block,
   cut into cubes

In a bowl, mix the rhubarb with the cornflour (cornstarch), then add the sugar, cardamom, lemon zest, orange juice and vanilla bean paste, and mix again.

Preheat the air fryer to 170°C (340°F). Tip the rhubarb into an ovenproof dish that fits your air fryer and air-fry for 15 minutes until the rhubarb is soft but still holding its shape. Carefully remove the cardamom pods and strip of lemon zest.

While the rhubarb is cooking, mix together the oats, sugar, flour, polenta and orange zest for the crumble topping. Rub the cubed vegan block into the flour mixture, using your fingertips, until you have a rubbly sand texture.

Once the rhubarb has had its time, scatter the crumble topping over the rhubarb and return to the air fryer for 6 minutes until the top is golden brown and slightly crispy.

Serve with big scoops of ice cream.

Serves 4
–
Prep 15 mins
–
Cook 21 mins

SPICED BREAD & BUTTER PUDDING

You'll need a cake tin (pan), about 6cm (2½in) deep, for this. Make sure it fits inside your air fryer but doesn't touch the heating element at the top. My husband loves this recipe so much that he eats any leftovers for breakfast. Why not?

pinch of saffron strands
1 tbsp boiling water
60g (2¼oz) unsalted butter, softened
6 slices of day-old white bread
75g (2½oz) dried cranberries, raisins or
    sultanas (golden raisins) or a mixture
3 medium eggs
3 tbsp soft light brown sugar
200ml (7fl oz/scant 1 cup) whole milk
250ml (8½fl oz/1 cup) double
    (heavy) cream
1 tsp vanilla bean paste
1 tsp ground cinnamon
fresh grating of nutmeg

Put the saffron in a small heatproof bowl, add the boiling water and leave to steep for 10 minutes.

Butter both sides of each slice of bread and slice them all in half diagonally. Layer the triangular slices in a deep 20cm (8in) cake tin (pan), scattering the dried fruit as you go. A deep tin is best, so the custard doesn't leak out. Set aside.

In a bowl, whisk together the eggs, sugar, milk, cream, vanilla bean paste, cinnamon, nutmeg and soaked saffron (along with the soaking water) until smooth and combined. Pour this mixture over the layered bread and press the top slices down slightly. Leave the bread to soak up the liquid for 10–15 minutes.

Preheat the air fryer to 170°C (340°F). Air-fry the pudding for 18 minutes until golden brown on top and custardy in the middle.

This is best eaten warm, but is also delicious cold the following day.

Serves 4
–
Prep 25 mins
–
Cook 18 mins

BERRY CLAFOUTIS

This is like a big berry pancake and is traditionally made in an oven. It's best made in a shallow stainless steel or enamel dish so you can bring it to the table. Allow it to sit for 10 minutes before serving up – you'll need a knife and a serving spoon to help scoop it out.

80g (2¾oz) unsalted butter, melted
300g (10½oz) fresh or frozen berries (a mixture of raspberries, cherries, blueberries, redcurrants and blackberries work well), defrosted if frozen
30g (1oz) plain (all-purpose) flour
4 tbsp ground almonds
80g (2¾oz) caster (superfine) sugar
3 medium eggs
150ml (5fl oz/⅔ cup) whole milk
1 tsp vanilla bean paste

To serve
fresh ricotta
icing (confectioners') sugar

Preheat the air fryer to 180°C (350°F).

Brush 15g (½oz) of the melted butter over the base and sides of a 20cm (8in) square ovenproof dish, about 5cm (2in) deep, then scatter the berries over the base of the dish.

In a bowl, whisk together the flour, ground almonds, sugar and eggs until combined, then add the milk, vanilla bean paste and remaining melted butter, until you have a completely smooth batter. Pour this over the berries and place in the air fryer for 35 minutes until the batter has puffed up a little around the berries.

Remove and leave to sit for a couple of minutes before serving slices or spoonfuls, with some ricotta on the side and a sprinkle of icing (confectioners') sugar.

Serves 4
–
Prep 10 mins
–
Cook 35 mins

ROASTED PLUMS WITH GINGER & PISTACHIOS VE

Warm, heavily spiced plums are just as good for breakfast with some yogurt as they are for pudding. This is also great served cold or at room temperature. The recipe works just as well with under-ripe plums, so you can enjoy it before the season is in full swing.

12 plums, halved and stones removed
6 tbsp maple syrup
2 tsp ground mixed (pumpkin pie) spice
2 star anise
5cm (2in) piece of fresh root ginger, finely grated
1 tsp vanilla bean paste

To serve
50g (1¾oz) pistachios, roughly chopped
vegan double (heavy) cream (a coconut variety works well)

Preheat the air fryer to 180°C (350°F), removing the crisper plate.

In a bowl, mix the plums with the maple syrup, mixed spice, star anise, ginger and vanilla bean paste. Pour everything onto the base of the air-fryer basket so the plums sit in a single layer. (If you're using an oven-style air fryer or one with a perforated basket, use an ovenproof dish that fits your air fryer.) Roast for 18 minutes, turning halfway through, until soft and syrupy.

Remove from the air fryer and leave to cool to room temperature.

Serve with the pistachios sprinkled over the top, with some cream on the side.

Makes 6–8
–
Prep 10 mins
–
Cook 18 mins

INDEX

ACKNOWLEDGEMENTS

Firstly, I'd like to thank my mum's stainless-steel dishes. They're easily over 40 years old and work like they were made yesterday; they fitted perfectly into my air fryer and gave me a connection with her while I was writing. You might notice them in some of the photographs throughout this book.

Thank you to Chris, my husband. Never one to chuck away good food however old or mouldy it may have become; he bravely ate his way through all the recipes that didn't quite make the grade.

Thanks, as always, to my family and friends who keep the show on the road while I'm buried in annotated pieces of paper and have endless recipes to test. To my children – Joni, Wilbur, Gabriel and Clara – thanks for never taking me too seriously and for having busy, exciting lives of your own.

Thank you to my assistants, Christina, Lu, Jemima and Sarah, who made all the recipes alongside me on the shoot and kept everything clean and tidy! Your job can be underappreciated and underpaid, but I truly valued all your hard work and care when it came to preparing ingredients, packing away equipment, unpacking food deliveries, organizing the fridge and happily rushing off to find something we'd run out of.

Thank you to Rita – I loved spending time with you and shooting this book together. I loved learning about tones and colours from you and getting into all those special chats – I particularly enjoyed the singing and whistling while we worked! Max – props stylist extraordinaire – I'm in awe of your detailed eye and sense of what works for a particular dish. I don't know how you choose from all of those thousands of props!

Thanks to designer Katy, who was a joy to hang out with while we took the photos (although I mostly want to thank you for introducing me to those insanely good chocolate-covered pretzels!). To Stacey, my commissioning editor, thank you for asking me to write this book – I've really enjoyed it. To Harriet, my editor, thank you for keeping me on track and on time (not one of my strong points). And to Sally, thank you for noticing all the important details I had missed and for the lovely chats over the phone. I hope we can all work together again on another book soon.